The Hitler Conspirator

The Hitler Conspirator

The Story of Kurt Freiherr von Plettenberg and
Stauffenberg's *Valkyrie* Plot to Kill the Führer

Eberhard Schmidt

With the assistance of
Dorothea-Marion von Plettenberg and
Karl-Wilhelm von Pletteberg

Foreword by
Peter Hoffmann F.R.S.C.

Translated by
Cordula Weschkun

FRONTLINE BOOKS

THE HITLER CONSPIRATOR
The Story of Kurt Freiherr von Plettenberg and Stauffenberg's
Valkyrie Plot to Kill the Führer

Original German language edition entitled *Kurt von Plettenberg. Im Kreis der Verschwörer um Stauffenberg Ein Lebensweg*, published by F.A. Herbig Verlagsbuchhandlung GmbH in 2014.

This English edition first published in 2016 by Frontline Books
an imprint of Pen & Sword Books Ltd,
47 Church Street, Barnsley, S. Yorkshire, S70 2AS
www.frontline-books.com

ISBN: 978-1-47385-691-2

CIP data records for this title are available from the British Library

Printed and bound by CPI Group (UK) Ltd, Croydon, CR0 4YY
Typeset in 10.5/13 point Palatino

For more information on our books, please email:
info@frontline-books.com,
write to us at the above address, or visit:
www.frontline-books.com

Contents

Foreword

This biography honours one of Germany's extraordinary personages, as those who knew him maintained. He fought in the retreat battles of 1918 in the Potsdam First Guard Regiment on Foot, refused to join a saber-fighting student fraternity and trained as a boxer instead, studied and administered forestry for noble landowners in East Prussia and in the Prussian and Reich governments, served in the Polish and Russian campaigns in 1939 and 1941, eventually in 1942 became plenipotentiary manager and president of the estate of the former Royal House of Prussia (Hohenzollernsche Verwaltung). He was among the conspirators who met at Carl-Hans Count Hardenberg's Neuhardenberg estate and belonged to the circle that included Axel Baron von dem Bussche, Fritz-Dietlof Count von der Schulenburg and Claus Schenk Count von Stauffenberg, and he participated in the preparation of an assassination attack upon Hitler and the planning of the coup d'état. When investigations finally led to his arrest on 3 March 1945 and he was threatened with torture if he refused to name other conspirators, he knocked down his interrogator on 10 March with a right hook and threw himself out of a fourth floor window to his instant death. Eberhardt Schmidt's biography is a captivating account of Plettenberg's life and of this extraordinary personage.

He was not alone, of course, as a list of anti-Hitler conspirators demonstrates, all of whom risked and hundreds of whom gave their lives to bring down the monster. But though they were many, they were not numerous enough to halt the orgies of murder and destruction. It was not they, and it was not the other rational and reasonable citizens who set the course of events at crucial junctures, but narrow coteries of inner circles. These were not answerable to public and transparent authorities and bodies, such as elected people´s representatives, or even judges in a state court (Staatsgerichtshof).

In Germany the Emperor William II in July 1914 decided with his war minister, his army chief of staff, the head of his military cabinet, his adjutant general, a captain of the naval staff, an admiral of the naval secretariat of state, the chancellor and the foreign secretary whether or not to promise Austria-Hungary support in case Russia intervened against her over Serbia.[i] It was thus, too, in the Russian Empire, the Austro-Hungarian Empire, and in the Republic of France. Each of the three emperors and the French president could have said "no"; if only one of them had said "no", if France had warned Russia that it would not support Russian military intervention in the Balkans, there would have been very little likelihood of war. Even in the United Kingdom the King could have said "no", while the House of Commons did not get to vote on war or peace until the Kingdom was in the war. Even in the British parliamentary monarchy, decent and rational people who were not ministers had practically no influence. An exception might have been the editor of a national newspaper. But large parts of the involved nations and their elected representatives were already in military confrontation mode. Where parliamentary votes were taken, they supported the war. In Germany, too, on 4 August 1914, even the socialists, including their radical Left, voted for the war appropriations.

Instead of having the opportunity to opt for diplomacy and negotiation, the nations, apart from the inner coteries, had no say. Given their gender, age and fitness they were obliged to serve and kill the designated "enemies"—people like themselves. In sum, people´s lives were not their own, people´s lives were managed for them to the utmost extent. After the war, they were left alone to deal with the consequences.

In January 1933, again, a decision for war was taken by persons unanswerable to any scrutiny by parliamentary or other representative or supervisory authorities. Again, a person in authority, this time the president of the German Republic, Paul von Hindenburg, could have said "no", and very likely there would not have been a Second World War. As it happened, a former chancellor, the state secretary in the Office of the Reich President, a banker and the president's son Oskar von Hindenburg conspired to smuggle Adolf Hitler into the chancellorship. Hindenburg wanted an end to political turmoil and no more elections. Hitler's lie that he could form a cabinet based on majority support in parliament (Reichstag) convinced the President. Hindenburg enabled Hitler to establish a dictatorship, "in the interest of safeguarding the German nation". But Hitler's appointment meant war, as he had been indicating in public speeches and as he himself declared to the Reichswehr leadership four days after his appointment.

Again, the powers that be were going to force eligible men into military service and combat against enemies who had not attacked Germany.

For people whose values were justice, peace and non-violence, it was impossible to do right, unless they fled their country. Failing that, Hitler was able not only to unleash another murderous war, but also to force soldiers into complicity in the most horrible crimes in recent human history. Kurt Baron von Plettenberg confronted the evil and gave his life as a result.

Peter Hoffmann
McGill University, Montreal

---

[i] The Chancellor, Theobald von Bethmann Hollweg; the Foreign Ministry's State Secretary, Arthur Zimmermann; the Minister of War, Erich von Falkenhayn; the head of the Emperor's Military Cabinet, Moriz von Lyncker; the Emperor's Adjutant-General, Hans von Plessen; Captain Hans Zenker of the Naval Staff; Admiral Eduard von Capelle of the Naval State Secretariat.

Preface

'I do not fear death, for I will have a fair judge'

When Kurt Freiherr von Plettenberg returned to Cecilienhof Castle in Potsdam on 24 July 1944, four days after the failed attempt on Hitler's life, he found 'on his desk, for all to see, the note of a telephone call: "Colonel Count Stauffenberg requests Baron Plettenberg to drive with him to Neuhardenberg at 2pm on 19th July"'. This was a coded message telling him that the last stage of Operation *Valkyrie* had begun. Thanks to his loyal staff the Gestapo knew nothing of this. Immediate arrest would have been the certain consequence.

Plettenberg, the plenipotentiary of the former royal house of Prussia, was one of the few members of the conspiracy's inner circle who was not interrogated or arrested by the Gestapo in the weeks that followed. Eberhard Zeller wrote: 'Unexpectedly, he who had met with Stauffenberg frequently during the previous weeks remained free.' When he finally was arrested by the Gestapo at the beginning of March 1945 after a denunciation, and brought to the infamous prison at Prinz-Albrecht- Straße 8 in Berlin, many of his co-conspirators had already been tried by the People's Court and executed. During interrogations he was threatened with torture, if he did not give up other conspirators. After that, during a grilling on the fourth floor of the prison, he punched the officer questioning him on the chin and threw himself out of the window. He was killed instantly.

Kurt von Plettenberg, the father of three small children, had preferred suicide to the danger of betraying his friends and allies.

The last message conveyed to his widow read: 'I do not fear death, for I will have a fair judge. Will my family be provided for? Please give the apple and the cigarettes still in my possession to the guard who always was so kind to me.'

Who was this man of the ancient Westphalian nobility, to whom – at the decisive moment – his own life and the consideration of his family meant less than saving the lives of his friends and allies and preserving his self-respect? Where did the resolve come from to set himself against the majority of Germans, among them most of his peers, who cheered Adolf Hitler in the years after 1933 and followed him into his criminal war adventure?

This account of his life begins with his upbringing in a Prussian Protestant family of the Wilhelmine era, and continues with his experiences as a machine-gun officer during the First World War to his professional career as Senior State Forester and general agent of the former Prussian royal family. Only with this background can his path to resistance against the Third Reich, including his decision to take his own life, be understood.

This book is dedicated to his memory.

Chapter 1

The Prussian Heritage

Kurt von Plettenberg came from a very old Westphalian noble family. As early as 1042 a knight named von Plettenberg is mentioned as the participant in a tournament in Halle. The most famous bearer of that name was Wolter von Plettenberg, the later Landmeister of the Teutonic Knights in Livonia. Emperor Charles V elevated him to the rank of an Imperial Prince. Under his leadership, the unified Livonia's army of knights, landsknechts and peasants twice prevailed, in 1501 and 1502, over the numerically far superior army of the Muscovite Grand Duke Ivan III, with whom he later concluded a peace lasting for almost sixty years. Since the nineteenth century the male members of the Plettenberg-Stockum line, of which Kurt von Plettenberg's family was a part, always chose a military career. Eugen Baron von Plettenberg, Kurt's grandfather, was a major and squadron commander in the 8th Westphalian Hussars. Kurt's father, Karl von Plettenberg, also started his career in the Prussian military.

In order to understand what it meant to be born into an old noble family at the end of the nineteenth century, it is helpful to examine this 'noblesse' more closely. At that time the nobility was still strictly set apart from the ascendant bourgeoisie by its lifestyle and values. The centre of the nobility's way of life was the family unit with its long tradition, within which the individual member was a link in a firmly-established chain, obliged to contribute to its standing, preservation and continuity. On the basis of marriages as evenly matched as possible, far-reaching kinship ties were wrapped around the inner family circle, which

1

acted as social networks and supported family members in crisis. Furthermore, an extensive range of connections was cultivated by the officers in particular, which later were of great importance for the network established by the resistance.

In contrast to the middle-class concept of life, which viewed the development of individuality and the increase of education and knowledge as the prerequisite for the desired social and economic advancement, the young nobles were prepared for a leadership role in the state. From the nurturing of strength of character, the appropriate conduct between the sexes, table manners and bearing resulted in codes by which they recognised and valued each other. More important than gaining specialist knowledge – 'one is already someone by birth' – was preparation for practical activity. As late as 1926 Ewald von Kleist-Schmenzin wrote in his essay *Nobility and Spirit of Prussia*: 'The pursuit of intellectuality has to find its limits there where it thrives at the expense of the rounded personality, deep rootedness and force of action.'

That does not mean that the nobility did not value education. The vast majority of their sons attended grammar schools or select private schools, took general qualifications for university entrance and began studies with a particular concentration on law, agriculture and forestry. They studied at a few select universities where, as a rule, they became members of exclusive fraternities, which strengthened their social position. Unlike the middle classes, their studies were not for the purposes of social advancement but rather to qualify them for the management and preservation of the family estates.

Most of their daughters, in contrast, received a less intellectually-challenging education, limited to preparing them for their later duties as wives and ladies of the house and for charitable work. Knowledge of foreign languages was taught to enable perfect conversation. Likewise housekeeping, dancing, gymnastics, music and painting served to improve their marriage prospects. Apart from a few exceptions, they did not use these skills professionally.

The lifestyle of most Prussian Protestant noble families was somewhat spartan, in contrast to the Catholic nobles of Southern Germany who as a rule owned larger estates. Children were not spoilt, and a 'culture of frugality' was cultivated. Thrift, simplicity, austerity, obedience and severity were viewed as great values. 'Be more than you seem' was the motto. The children were taught the 'Prussian' virtues of duty, incorruptibility, a sense of justice, decency, integrity, and reliability. On this basis, Prussia had developed a very progressive legal system and an efficient administration, on which the citizens could rely and within the framework of which industry and trade flourished before the First World War.

Beyond this, so it seems from many later childhood memories of these generations, noble masculinity was defined by character, in the sense of total control of the body and emotions till contempt for death. At the same time the notion of superiority was cherished, which also included the acceptance of responsibility. These challenges to character and behaviour were felt the more urgently, the more one could feel part of one's class only through behaviour fitting one's rank, rather than through possession of estates, and thus could prove oneself worthy of tradition.

The value of honour and the duty of politeness towards the opposite sex completed the educational ideal. It is the image of the knight which influenced the ideal of an education befitting the nobility's standing. In the schools of the nobility, the model of the 'modern knight' included music and dancing (also for the men), horse riding and fencing besides lessons in military science and drill. Martial and courtly elements in the shape of a civilised, even sophisticated enjoyment of life seem to be reconcilable with each other. In the exterior form the internal attitude ought to be reflected.

Although the nobility, whether they had land or not, were in an increasingly defensive position as regards the rising middle classes, they asserted their political and social hegemony for a long time, at least until 1918. If we examine the relationship between the nobility and the bourgeoisie in Prussia's leading officer corps, still in 1912 in regiments such as the 1st Foot Guards all eighty-six officers were nobles, despite the trend towards professionalisation of the military. The same held true for the 3rd Guard Uhlans stationed in Potsdam. In only a few other guards regiments did middle-class officers reach significant numbers or even surpassed the number of noble officers. In the General Staff three out of four officers were of noble descent. The noble officer was the social role model of Wilhelmine society, recognised and imitated by the upper middle class, despite the contempt for civilian matters often displayed by the nobility.

* * *

The men of the Plettenberg family were also raised towards this idea, including Kurt's father, Karl von Plettenberg. According to Georg von dem Bussche, he must have been a colourful character, a 'roughneck with a heart'. Born in 1852 in Neuhaus near Paderborn, he had been intended for the career of a Prussian officer since childhood. Early on, his father had taken him along to the barracks and on the hunt. Of his three siblings the second oldest, Eugen, died at the age of 18. His sisters Jenny and Minette married within their social class. The young Karl had an extremely strict Protestant upbringing. In his 'memoirs' he talks of a tutor, the candidate Heinrich Vogel, son of a blacksmith, 'externally little favoured, but also his inner humanity could probably not be detected. Nevertheless I felt a kind of affection in my heart, yet at any rate gratitude towards him, for he understood to drum the basics of the sciences into me in the truest sense of the word – on average he broke a stick a day on my back – so that I could be accepted into the 6th year of the cadet school in May 1864 at the age of eleven.' Corporal punishment was customary at that time. The regime in the cadet schools was extremely harsh and the methods of education quite brutal.

When Karl von Plettenberg turned fourteen, he enrolled in the cadet school in Bensberg, transferring two years later to the main cadet school in Berlin-Lichterfelde to obtain his degree. The 18-year-old served in the war against France as an ensign and lieutenant, and in 1871 witnessed the proclamation of Emperor Wilhelm I at Versailles. The foundation of the German Empire influenced his whole life. After the war Karl von Plettenberg studied at the Prussian Military Academy in Berlin. With this his professional path is predestined. Found suitable as a troop leader, he joins the 'Leibkompanie' of the 1st Foot Guard Regiment in Potsdam, one of the conditions for which is that the man be at least 1.87m tall. Soon he became a company commander, and as he was a passionate hunter, the officer corps elects him as master of the hunt. Furthermore 'Plettenaugust' – his nickname within the regiment and later also at the veterans' reunions – was leader of the dance at court for a long time. During his time in the 1st Foot Guard Regiment he met the future Emperor Wilhelm II in the officers' mess. The prince was also a company commander in the regiment. This comradeship might have contributed to his later becoming the emperor's aide-de-camp and finally his adjutant-general. The hunt and the outdoor life were an escape from the world of cadet schools, barracks and officers' messes, which he loved very much. The same preferences were later shown by his son Kurt.

At the age of 33, he became engaged to the 21-year-old Clara Countess von Wedel who also came from Westphalia, from House Sandfort in Münsterland. Her father was Royal Prussian Chamberlain, a district magistrate and a retired colonel. Clara was a distant relative of Plettenberg, as her mother Luise was a descendent of the Bodelschwingh-Plettenberg branch of the family. She was the sole survivor of the family's eight children. After the wedding in 1887 the young couple moved into a small apartment at the Luisenplatz in Potsdam, near the Brandenburg Gate and the park of Sanssouci. Meanwhile, Karl von Plettenberg had been promoted to captain.

According to the understanding of a woman's role at that time, Clara von Plettenberg led a private existence. It was characteristic of the marginal role of women in these circles, typical of the period, that the birth of Kurt is only mentioned in passing in her father's house book. She only rarely occurs in the 'memoirs' of her husband, too. However, during Karl's absence in the First World War the couple maintained a constant correspondence which reveals their deep bond. Karl was clearly very attached to his gentle wife Clara. It is passed on in the family that he paced back and forth restlessly, if Clara was late. As Karl von Plettenberg was an irascible man, in later years his wife with her soothing nature had to mediate time and again in arguments between the father and his oldest son, Karl-Wilhelm. The first son Walter, born in February 1888, had died in Potsdam four months after his birth.

Then in 1889 the eagerly anticipated son and heir Karl-Wilhelm was born.

In 1890 the General Staff ordered Karl von Plettenberg's transfer to Bückeburg. He was promoted to major and became commander of the 7th Light Infantry Battalion, the 'Bückeburger Jäger'. From his memoirs we can see how difficult the Plettenbergs found leaving Potsdam and Berlin:

> On 21st March 1890 we had had some close acquaintances over for dinner from whom we parted late, after my prospects of becoming aide-de-camp had been discussed once more in detail. No sooner had they left, when a throng of young officers spilled through the Brandenburg Gate with terrible shouting from which I could only understand 'Bückeburg' again and again. Imagine my dismay when it became finally clear that I was indeed transferred to the 7th Light Infantry Battalion in Bückeburg while being promoted to major. We felt expelled from paradise and were deeply unhappy. The idea of exchanging the handsome uniform of the 1st Guard Regiment for that of a light infantry battalion and in particular having to wear the ugly shako was terrible. The parting from my company was extremely difficult for me. After years I still cried when I heard the Torgauer March which my dear lads sang so beautifully. How willingly I would have foregone promotion, if I had been able to lead my company again. And yet my promotion to major ahead of

time was the turning-point in my military advancement and the reason for having gained the higher positions at a relatively young age ... Prince Friedrich Leopold took over my company. He was without any military experience. My dear, faithful lads had to suffer much due to this in the subsequent company drills.

It took some time for the Plettenbergs to feel at home in Bückeburg. In those days it was a placid little town, located in beautiful scenery, but they were used to the splendour of the Potsdam court. Of course, a Prussian officer – even of high rank – had to be content with a rather modest salary as a rule, which enabled the family to live according to their social standing, but not in luxury. Prussia rewarded with the honour and distinction of the rank. If there was no private income, as was the case with the Plettenbergs, the aforementioned 'culture of frugality' becomes the guideline of daily life. Kurt von Plettenberg's rejection of a materialist orientation in life has its roots in this context.

The family rented a modest apartment on the first floor above the court pharmacy opposite the castle at the town's marketplace. The members of the princely house of Schaumburg-Lippe seem rather strange to Karl von Plettenberg. He describes them with humour:

> To a greater or lesser extent, the 'very princely' ladies and gentlemen of the ruling house had peculiar personalities. The nearly 80-year-old prince who had been in the 8th Hussar Regiment with my late father received me with the greatest cordiality; as it was revealed later, however, this did not extend so far as to satisfy my passion for hunting which was still burning at that time. He himself was a very passionate, distinguished hunter and excellent marksman ... Among the prince's four sons Prince Hermann, who had participated in the war of 1870/71 as a member of the battalion and wore the uniform of the 7th Jäger, stood out in particular through his

original character. His avowed passion was breeding chickens, his particular project being to breed chicken in the colours of Schaumburg-Lippe [white-red-blue]. He always carried chicken feed in his pockets and thus gave off a very peculiar smell. He claimed not to be able to sit in chairs due to health reasons. Therefore he had installed a wooden horse in his rooms and the lounge car of the train, on which he rode … When it rained on the Emperor's birthday, he appeared on horseback in parade uniform with an umbrella. For the commander he was a great burden, because he cross-examined the younger officers and reported everything to his 'very princely' father.

On official service much patience was required:

On the first day of each month, the commander had to report to the supreme chief, the prince. I was ordered to do so at 12; however, as everybody knew, since the prince never rose before 1pm, you had to anticipate a great length of time waiting. The distinguished gentleman appeared as he had risen from the bed – literally – in a dressing gown and slippers, beneath it only underwear and socks, and he often engaged me for hours with the discussion of the most trivial matters. My predecessor claimed that such a reception in the 'coronation cloak', as he called the outfit, was proof of special favour.

The old prince died in 1893. When he had become seriously ill, the doctors had a tough job with him because he would not follow their instructions.

His successor, Prince Georg, was described by Karl von Plettenberg as a gracious superior, 'whom we all came to love soon after; under the influence of his youthful, fun-loving wife a lively society developed so that the little residence was soon unrecognisable … Finally we felt at home in small Bückeburg and recognised what importance a small court has for town and country.'

* * *

Kurt Eugen Gustav Adolf Baron von Plettenberg was born on 31 January 1891 in Bückeburg as the second son of this Prussian noble family. In 1894 the family was recalled to Potsdam by the emperor who appointed Plettenberg his aide-de-camp. Kurt's childhood and youth in the bosom of his family show many traits typical for the nobility. Here the influence of the father is of particular importance. Only one day a year were Karl-Wilhelm and Kurt allowed to be 'cheeky' to their father, otherwise they have to obey.

Kurt's cousin, Elisabeth von Sydow, who was nine years older, would later become his intimate 'little cousin', recalled him as a 'three-year-old little boy, head covered in blonde curls … Kurt was a general favourite due to his cheerful and tender manner', a trait which he kept as a grown man, as we know from the testament of his friends. About the young Kurt Plettenberg she remembered: 'He read well and widely and had an astonishing memory, loved poetry which he could recite well, too.' His cheerfulness was proverbial. The upbringing by his parents was Protestant, emphatically loyal to the emperor and stressing the love for the fatherland.

His mother's influence in this upbringing cannot be adequately appreciated due to the lack of sources. According to accounts of Kurt's future wife, her mother-in-law Clara had a talent for lyric poetry which she was unable to develop, however, because of her duties at her husband's side. Yet it is very likely that her son Kurt's love for poetry can be traced back to his mother's influence. Kurt was very attached to his mother all his life. In his correspondence with her, especially during the First World War, he avoided worrying her, as all soldiers do, and demonstrated his attachment to her. As with so many families, it was the mother, who herself had grown up with nine siblings, who took care that the ties within the extended family were preserved and filled with life. Her influence on the upbringing of her two sons and her younger daughter Luise cannot be understated.

Kurt learnt from early on to conduct himself in a manner 'befitting his rank' and to internalise the values connected with that. This becomes clear not least through the pictures hanging in the family's living room. The one picture shows Wolter von Plettenberg, the Landmeister of the Teutonic Order in Livonia, and the other the Bamberger Reiter, the embodiment of chivalrous 'modesty' and 'virtue'. The ideal of a 'knight in shining armour' stayed with Kurt von Plettenberg all his life. It points, aside from 'chivalrous behaviour' to one's fellow men, mainly to the traditional Christian care for the weak and needy. Providing help to them is viewed as a significant aspect of daily life.

As the second son Kurt was spared his father's cadet school, as only his older brother Karl-Wilhelm was intended for a military career. So from 1900 to 1906 Kurt attended the grammar schools in Potsdam and Charlottenburg. In August 1900 his sister Luise was born. Meanwhile, his father had been promoted to lieutenant-colonel and commander of the famous 1st Foot Guards whose motto 'Semper Talis' still adorns the gate of their former barracks in Potsdam today.

Appointed inspector of the huntsmen and marksmen in 1902, Karl von Plettenberg had responsibility for the Mounted 'Feldjäger' Corps, created by Frederick the Great in 1740 for reconnaissance and courier duties. Its veterans were taken on by the Prussian Forest Service. Meanwhile, the corps had developed from a military educational institution into an organisation for recruitment to the Prussian forestry service, the forestry component of the training finally coming to outweigh the military one. Lieutenants or senior lieutenants in the 'Feldjäger' complete a course in forestry and remain in the corps until a position as a senior forestry official becomes available.

In 1906 Karl von Plettenberg became commander of the 22nd Division in Kassel, a post he held for four years. For the brothers

Karl-Wilhelm and Kurt the years spent in Kassel are a particularly happy time. The boys, growing into independence, are often invited on holiday by relatives and friends who still possess estates. In 1910 they passed their *Abitur* (university entrance exam) there, both with very good grades, which especially pleased their father given his public position, as he expressly noted in his memoirs.

Given paternal influence, it is not surprising that Kurt decides to join the forestry service. It was not least his marked love for nature which predestined him for it. All his life, nature was a source from which he could draw strength time and again, especially in times of crisis, be it during stalking and hunting, during walks with friends or simply experiencing its magnificence. At first hunting was his primary passion – as was already the case with his father – and he noted down, also in his later diaries, game, tracking, the joy he feels, or the occasional missed shot. Yet he was too versatile to merely concentrate on forestry and hunting.

To become a forester at that time, an individual needed to complete a demanding university course. After two terms at the universities of Kiel and Lausanne, where he primarily attended lectures in law, he applied to the Prussian Forest Service and was accepted in spring 1911. The customary half-year apprenticeship was undertaken in the forestry office of Menz, steeped in tradition, near Stechlin in Brandenburg. In October his military service followed, the 'one year voluntary service' which he fulfilled with the 18th (2nd Grand Ducal Mecklenburgian) Dragoon Regiment in Parchim. Subsequently Kurt spent a further four terms at the forestry academy in Hannoversch-Münden. In between he worked his way through the obligatory military exercises to qualify him as a reserve officer. He declined membership in a fencing fraternity. In order not to be considered a coward, but also because of the strength training involved, he takes boxing lessons and later wins the army championship in his weight class.

His father was appointed commanding general of the IX Army Corps in Altona in 1912, and in 1913 took command of the Guards

Corps to which all Royal Prussian Army Guard regiments belong. The family was now at the highest levels of Wilhelmine society.

In 1914 the First World War interrupted Kurt's studies. The outbreak of the war surprised the brothers Karl-Wilhelm and Kurt, despite all the signs which at least since 1913 pointed to a confrontational resolution of the tensions between the major powers in Europe. They had to postpone their plans for a great African trip, which they had already prepared in great detail.

Chapter 2

Lieutenant in
the First World War

The brothers Kurt and Karl-Wilhelm von Plettenberg joined the war with great enthusiasm, like so many of their peers and educated middle-class youth. The young soldiers firmly believed in the emperor and Germany's mission.

Kurt, 23 years old in August 1914, at the time only saw that the entry into war meant farewell to a carefree youth. He deals almost playfully with the possibility of death and thanks his favourite cousin as a representative of his extended family for his happy years growing up.

Participation in the war seems to him virtually an obligatory duty in thanks for that:

> My dearest Elisabeth,
> ... I have remained the old optimist, both for our people – although I realise the terrible seriousness of the situation – and also for me personally. Yet one has to bring to mind the possibility that it might be a long goodbye which I say to you per letter. Now I would like ... to express my heartfelt gratitude to you for everything I owe you in my youth, for the innumerable happy and cosy hours in Westhusen and Himmighausen. How much I enjoyed being at your place, – I believe you already know this. – Going to war seems to me my personal duty out of gratitude. Now we have to earn

retrospectively everything that we were able to enjoy undeservedly throughout Germany thanks to so many dear persons, especially in our family. ... KW [his brother Karl-Wilhelm] is in Hans Bock's company about which we are all very glad. I have become a Second Uhlan, unfortunately not in the cavalry division where Spatz, Kurd, Gisbert, Moritz and all the good lads are, but if we are not 'switched off' immediately, we will probably meet in the field ... Salvation and victory!

Karl-Wilhelm went to war in an even more euphoric mood. After Liège was taken under Ludedorff's command on 7 August he crows on a postcard to his brother Kurt:

Hurray!
Stormed Liège!
Boy!
It is splendid!
Off to Walhalla!

Karl-Wilhelm also communicates his exuberant enthusiasm to his aunt Erika:

My dear aunt Erika!
... We go to battle! Oh, it is wonderful! You cannot know how overwhelming the exaltation presents itself throughout Germany. Hundreds of thousands flock zealously to the flag, all singing and rejoicing; the victorious cheer rings though the city due to the storming of Liège! Our squads are filled with a wonderful spirit, the officer corps serious and restrained, as it is fitting in the face of such an enormous task, and yet in every heart dwells the blazing joy that we are allowed to take part and experience this great hour!
It seems to us all the fulfilment of our longing and endeavours!!! The fruits will show themselves in the field. I

have only this one wish that I will lead my proud grenadiers with honour against the enemy. Then I will gladly die, I face death calmly and controlled, and this is proof to me that I fought righteously.

If it has to be outside in the field, if many of us do not return, please think of the splendid old landsknecht song: no better death in the world than he who is struck down by the enemy, on the green meadow, on the wide field, must not hear great lament!!!

Everything is beauty and harmony; mankind seems to have risen above itself. Only the noblest of feelings propel the people forward! Oh century, it is a joy to live.

I believe, since the existence of the world no prouder and more enthusiastic unit under a more chivalrous leader has taken to the field than today the guard corps under my father. Naturally we have ended all quarrels. Such things vanish in the face of the dramatic greatness of the moment.

Hans, my company leader, Kurdel [Kurt, his brother] Second Guard Uhlan, that O. Dolf [Adolf Count v. Wedel, husband of Erika] is here, all this is very good. I did not see him, but he is in a place worthy of him. Be proud, and don't be sad. I firmly believe that as always you will face destiny with calm certainty! Now I have to conclude, I am exhausted!

Farewell, dearest aunty, again many, many thanks!!!

Although the youthful pathos of Wilhelmine society is perceived here, his last letter concluded with very personal foreboding:

What will the next weeks bring?
Victory and honour, I hope with confidence! – Or death!
I can accept both, death in the face of the enemy seems to me
a Germanic end to my life so filled with anxiety!
Farewell forever!
Your Karl-Wilhelm

On 29 August the Germans launched a large-scale attack on St Quentin in Picardy in the north of France. Karl-Wilhelm von Plettenberg, Lieutenant in the 1st Foot Guards, was killed on the same day by a grenade explosion during an attack on the French lines, as he was advancing with drawn sword at the head of his company. His father, the commanding general, personally searched for him on the battlefield and found his dead son. He buried him the next day with Kurt and many of his comrades in attendance. 'Walhalla', the residence and hall of fame of the fallen Germanic warriors invoked by Karl-Wilhelm, became the sad reality of death.

Kurt, at that time a 23-year-old lieutenant, mourns his beloved older brother deeply. His mother writes in October 1914 to Kurt's cousin Elisabeth:

> I now have, when I no longer have himself, at least the wonderful memories of the past 25 years and am grateful that he has acquitted himself well to the last; for Kurdel it is actually much harder, he was so attached to Karl-Wilhelm and with him has lost so much that he now feels boundlessly desperate, especially as he is no longer with the regiment among his contemporaries, but with the staff among only older officers.

Kurt's pride in the 'hero's death' of his brother was expressed in a letter to his mother from 1 November 1914, with which he supports himself, but also the belief in the unique possibility offered by the war to prove oneself in the face of death, quite different from peacetime:

> You write to me: 'For us only the painful loss remains – and too often a tale is told to us by invoking pride.' My dearest mother – this missing is indeed very painful, but I am nevertheless comforted by pride. I tell myself it is given to all of us who have entered the world to persist on the difficult

path until the end. For an average person it is very, very difficult to go on gaining honour and glory on this path. Otherwise we muddle through our everyday lives, towards death which reaches us with unshakable certainty. Also here some are befallen by death, who die heroically only in the eyes of the world, but whom fear gripped to the marrow and who only died because they had no alternative. Yet I understand a true hero's death – so it was for Karl-Wilhelm and thank God for most of our people by virtue of heritage – as a glad, confident facing and meeting of the grim reaper. It contains the will to show what cannot be shown (or only a little) during peace times; that one is internally free, that one has the strength to follow one's ideal until the last breath. Of this you should be proud.

Many of Kurt von Plettenberg's generation thought like him at the beginning of the war. Many years later – the First World War was long over – he questioned the reasons for his initial war fever:

Why did we boys view the war as salvation, why did we virtually blaze with happiness and joy? It was not ambition and the thirst for adventure, although some drops of both filled the cup of exaltation. I believe the reasons were two thoughts – to some these were unconscious, but the more perceptive and mature were entirely aware of them: firstly we strongly and confidently hoped that the focus of life for each of us was shifted from the pursuit of earnings, of advancement, of relentless working and operating, which was often enough considered an irksome duty – just like we viewed some lessons as schoolboys – to a great sphere for which we considered ourselves to be especially well suited due to tradition, blood and our own enthusiasm. And then – and this I very clearly recall of Karl-Wilhelm, but actually also of myself – we sensed or hoped for the possibility for a correction of the social injustice with which we were living. I myself have very often felt this as a proud awareness to be just a man amongst men, only enemy of the common enemy, due to my own voluntary commitment. I have found similar sentiments time and again in Flex and some others. And how much hoped for practical socialism [Sozialismus der Tat] have I seen in battle.

This attitude has been given a name: the 'Spirit of Langemarck'. If we follow the glorifying version, the young volunteers had charged in a death-defying manner towards the enemy's machine-gun positions in summer 1914 near Langemarck and had fallen in their thousands.

The little village in Flanders was subsequently made into the myth of a whole generation by the army command. Actually 'this strategically totally irrelevant attack' (Christoph Studt) was a military disaster. In order to 'cover up the reckless waste of human life', the war propaganda had to reinterpret the defeat as a moral victory.

When we read contemporary statements, time and again we encounter the war volunteers' belief that they were participating in something unique which went beyond the pursuit of earnings, advancement and security, often perceived as oppressive. The writer Bernhard von der Marwitz, of almost the same age, who fell in 1918 shortly before the end of the war, expressed it as follows: '… How different life has become all of a sudden. Who would have thought that it would suddenly become visible to all, this which had so long been our obscure belief, our secret hope, this great rising for a single great cause for the price of everything else …' With this something is addressed which moved many: the merging into a great structure, giving existence a meaning beyond petty purposes, a quasi-religious experience and a kind of awakening.

Aside from this uplifting sentiment another aspect defined the war experience: witnessing a social community. The shared experience at the front contributed to a levelling of social distinctions, often perceived as oppressive before the war. Plettenberg used for this the term 'practical socialism'. Here a desire to pull down the barriers of rank is indicated, an empathy with those who were worse off.

The philosopher Rudolph Eucken, very famous at that time and the first German winner of the Nobel Prize in Literature, also shared this hope for a beneficial social effect of the common front experience:

> Social ethics cannot find a more worthy embodiment than the context of an army where the fate of the one is tied immediately to that of the others, where the entire salvation of the individual depends on the progress of the whole, and where the individual is prepared every moment to sacrifice himself for the whole. Beyond the army, however, such an attitude encroaches upon the entire people as liberation from childish egoism and as voluntary commitment to the whole. Such elevation of the personality forms no contrast to the matter and its necessity; on the contrary its demands bring the people together and drive them to the most difficult achievements …

This conception of the organic dissolution of the individual into the whole is based on the experiences of the everyday routine of war, in the trenches of positional warfare where the soldiers and lower-ranking officers depended on each other without distinction of person or rank. Yet already towards the end of the war the old power structures and conflicts of interest re-emerged and led to the November Revolution, triggered by the mutiny of the sailors at Kiel. Despite everything, the hopes for greater social justice and equality were not fulfilled after the defeat of 1918.

* * *

On the Western Front the advance stalled as early as August 1914. The Battle of St Quentin had been the turning point. The German First Army was so hard-pressed by French and Belgian reserve units that its offensive was brought to a halt. The German troops changed their route and marched south towards the Marne and Paris. In September the Allies inflicted heavy losses on the Germans.

With the transition to trench warfare at the Marne in September it became clear that the Schlieffen plan had failed. The Chief of the General Staff von Moltke suffered a nervous breakdown and was replaced by the War Minister Erich von Falkenhayn. Falkenhayn still followed the offensive concept of his predecessor, but the positional warfare along a front of now more than 800km did no longer bring any significant advances. The advance of the Guard Corps finally ended 30km from Paris. The defenders had dug themselves in and held their lines.

Indicative of how this situation was covered up is an anecdote ascribed to Kurt's father, General of the Infantry:

> The troops, just having returned from a hard battle lasting several days, marched past me in flawless formation with tightly presented guns. From the last group of the rear guard a non-commissioned officer steps out, lowers the gun with perfect drill movement and addresses the following words to me: 'Does your excellency permit a question?' 'Yes!' 'Why do you retreat?' 'The others did not manage by themselves, we need to help.' With another perfect drill movement and the words 'My obedient thanks' the man steps back into formation.

The trench warfare on the Western Front lasted until shortly before the end of the war and claimed many victims on both sides in endless 'battles of material'. The German public, however, was misled by the supreme army command regarding the hopeless situation there with reports of victory. Later the so-called 'stab-in-the-back legend' was based on the self-same lies.

* * *

Already by the end of 1914 the General Staff reconsidered and shifted the focus of military deployment to the East. After fierce disputes within the General Staff the already-retired General Paul von Hindenburg and his chief of staff Erich Ludendorff, the 'conqueror of Liège', had taken over the supreme command in the East and had resoundingly beaten the superior Russian Army of the Narew at the Battle of Tannenberg at the end of August 1914, later also the Army of the Niemen. The Russians had to abandon East Prussia which they had occupied at the beginning of the war.

The young lieutenant Kurt von Plettenberg did not remain on the Western Front for long. Shortly after the outbreak of war, against his wishes he is appointed aide-de-camp on the staff of the 2nd Guard Division under the command of General von Winckler. He would rather have fought like his brother at the front where in his opinion he could have proved himself. In May 1915 Kurt was transferred with his regiment to the Eastern Front as part of reinforcements there and served as the commander of a machine-gun platoon in static battles against the Russian army.

His regiment advanced from Warsaw to Vilnius. In the course of this he encountered Eastern European Jewish culture for the first time and was impressed. On 8 May 1915 he wrote to his younger sister Luise about this experience:

> Jaslo, a small old town at the Wisloka river, the Jewish population in the most splendid getups, in most cases with long locks in black caftans. First I went to the synagogue where I took part in the thanksgiving service on the occasion of the liberation from the Russians, then the Emperor came to visit us and finally I travelled to my other quarters. The service was fabulously interesting and most likely as interesting as 2,000 years ago. I sat with two other officers at the front near the altar in a dignitaries' box to which we were led by the chief rabbi. Before us in a beautiful large synagogue pierced by several Russian shells about 600 Jews of all ages; below only men, above in the gallery the women! The chief rabbi sang loudly the whole time and now and then the entire choir joined in, either rejoicing or lamenting as required.

His respect for the Jews is also expressed in a later letter to his sister:

> If one seriously ponders religious questions, and not just as a mere intellectual exercise, then at first one finds many matters which seem wholly puzzling, but a person who has his heart in the right place will soon realise that all good people aim for the same goal and that only the paths are different ... So there are many people whose paths are diverting much farther from ours – Jews and professors – and yet many of them achieve much more than we will ever do.

From Vilnius the regiment was transported by train to Courland where Plettenberg's unit will spend the winter on occupation duties on the coast of the bay of Riga. On 11 October 1915 he tells his cousin Elisabeth of his experiences there:

> We were many weeks without postal communication ... almost 100 kilometres in the rear of the Russian main army near Vilnius and have spent many a strange day. We have caught Russian railway transports, seized convoys and finally had to evade a very clever counter-manoeuvre by the Russians. Thank God I have developed extraordinary luck. Three times the Russians stormed our positions with tremendous cheering – the two times they managed to break through they did not reach us, however, but halted roughly 1,000 metres away and I could retreat in time, the third time I could take part in the 'disposing'.

Once he even became the hunted. He reported to his parents that he had a noteworthy experience in Russia. At dawn he wanted to make contact with the neighbouring infantry. Yet these had already evacuated their positions without notifying the lancers. Only halfway between the two trenches he recognised the Russians and ran for his life for 200m amidst the random, but very intense enemy fire. 'Now I know how the rabbit must feel in the aim of my Browning gun.' Despite these episodes, remarkably his cheerfulness and his optimism were expressed again and again, although his war fever was beginning to ease. The young officer spoke of his dreams in a letter to Elisabeth and hoped for a speedy end of the war;

> You know, there are in general so many things which one would like to see and experience, and it is not at all easy to suppress looking to the future and the building of castles in the air. I believe this is impossible, we are too young to do so and one is always hoping. If the war lasts much longer, the prospects of experiencing peace dwindle, but you know that I am expecting peace very <u>soon</u> and secondly that I am a 'lucky person' …

Meanwhile, his machine-gun platoon had increased from thirty to seventy men, plus seventy horses and three machine guns. The well-being of his 'people' is very important to him, as shown in a letter to his sister from April 1915: 'I am dreading the winter slightly. Not because of myself, for that would be silly, but I am concerned for our people. How the poor fellows will suffer from the cold and wet! We have so infinitely many advantages and alleviations that we have to endure not half as much.' In his letters and his war diary he longed for the end of the war in March 1916. He now only saw himself in his responsibility for his comrades on the Western Front who in his opinion were in more of a mess than himself:

> What a peculiar frenzy this war is and what might be the actual original cause – I mean this philosophically and not politically or militarily – for the fact that the creator of the world allows it to happen! The sole comfort remains that after all war is nothing more than a long-term ration of all human misery for a short span of time. I hope for the Western Front!

The situation there must be unimaginable to outsiders, and I believe there will be men who will lose their minds because of it. Please do not think that I am crazy enough to long for such adventures. I have had absolutely enough of the war and would gladly march from here to Berlin. Yet should it be the case that I experience once more unpleasant atmospheric conditions, as they occasionally arise from so much flying lead, then I do not complain but am glad that I can pay off some of the debt to those who have been in constant battle for almost two years now. Therefore I always get going again gladly. To this the feeling is now added that my people have some skill, and since I have trained them, this is a rather pleasant feeling.

True to his optimistic nature, time and again he got something positive out of the war. In a letter from October 1915 he wrote:

My youth in the actual sense of the word is over. I have to slowly get used to this; but what I have learnt through the war is a good basis for work after the war and I look to the future with great confidence. We will not be spared disappointments, great or small, but I believe that we will reconcile ourselves with an unlimited number of much easier things, after we have been so emphatically directed to see the whole.

For him one of the wonderful things about the war was the experience of nature in Courland. His love for nature and the hunt, which he got from his father, had been there since childhood. It was an essential part of the development of his personality, influenced his choice of profession and would always remain a source of strength to him in the future, especially when he found himself in difficult circumstances. So he positively raves about the impressions offered by the Russian winter:

It is more beautiful here than you can actually imagine. We have Russian winter straight out of the picture book, and if you could see the incredibly large snow-covered fir and pine forests and the sea foaming in winter storms under the winter sun, you would cry out for the annexation of the Courland. The day before yesterday I strolled through a forest of firs. Imagine firs, birch and rowan trees – deep in snow, arranged in park-like groups; among them a deep brook; full moon and frosty snow glittering like gemstones. Where branches reached down in diamond arches, I would not have been surprised to glimpse erlkings and other fantastic sylvan majesties. You cannot conceive how beautiful it was.

Yet even during the quiet of positional warfare now and again dangerous situations arose. In November 1916 Plettenberg was been ordered with his platoon, which now has four machine guns, to Infantry Regiment (IR) 408. Its commander Siegfried zu Eulenburg later recounted how one quiet evening he was sitting with Plettenberg in front of a farm house playing chess. Suddenly Plettenberg got up and said to his baffled chess partner, balancing the board carefully: 'Come, let us rather go to the other side of the house.'

Half an hour later a shell hit the house and demolished the part where they had been sitting previously.

In general this part of the Eastern Front was quiet. War activities for the lieutenant were only the routine management of the positions and the changing of the horses. He used the time to send his 'heart's sister' Luise, nine years younger than him, admonitions and advice, but also wrote of his thoughts and worries.

On the occasion of her confirmation on 8 September 1915 he wrote:

> Dear little sister, believe me, I have spoken with many a good wise man who had to put an end to the outcome of his thoughts a hundred times a year in face of death, and by and by many a day have passed where I have thought back and forth in a searching, serious mood – they are always trivial

matters why people quarrel, if they have the one thing in common, the sacred, selfless will to do good!

On another occasion he confided his self-doubts to her, dressed up in humour:

> At the moment I have a habit to look for only good qualities in all people in order to improve my person and my achievements and to benefit from this. It has been a slight setback realising that I have found only very few people who accomplish less than me. Almost everybody has more skills and so often I envy my people, who at least know how to plough properly, to do carpentry and tailoring, while I stand to one side like a fool and painstakingly hide my absolute ignorance of all practical and theoretical matters behind a smattering of superficial education and diplomatic small talk.

He advises his sister to take care of her appearance, probably thinking of her future marriage. Usually in families of this class it was expected that the oldest daughter would look after the aging parents. Cousin Elisabeth has also remained unmarried for this reason. Later she will temporarily run the household of her younger cousin Kurt. Kurt's tender bond with his much younger sister becoming apparent from many letters suggests that the affectionate interaction with younger people, primarily girls, becomes a familiar pattern of relationships, also shaping his later attachments.

As he did not have to fight, Kurt von Plettenberg whiled away the time by swimming in the sea, riding, hunting and visiting the country seats of long-established Baltic barons. When reading his wartime diary the impression emerges that as the war went on he suffered greatly from the fact that he had no chance to show what he could do. He complained that positional warfare offered too few opportunities for self-improvement and to excel. An example of this is the entry on 7 July 1916, jotted down after home leave:

Now the short time at home is already behind me like a very calm, heavy dream and I am back up here once again – at war, as they say, but there is profound peace all around and we sense little of the war, much less than in Berlin. And in the east and west they are battling fiercely and bloodily, and I who hoped during peace to be allowed to stand where I belong, I have been sitting here and have to feel ashamed in front of 1,000 Jews and similar fellows who join in the fighting, while I shoot deer. It looks as if the decision will come soon; for the first time since the beginning of the war I have this feeling and now I am supposed to sit here for weeks and look on during our battle for existence. That is not pleasant and there is little honour in it. I believe this feeling will not leave me for my whole life.

This feeling increased as the war continued. A year later he confided to his diary:

The second half of July is like the first. I swim a lot and hope that the fatherland will need us, too. It seems to be a curse that I shall be a spectator during the war, and it is so difficult not to give up personally, to struggle with oneself, when one has nothing to do which keeps oneself occupied or rather demands one's whole attention. I have been sitting here since August 1915 and watching the war and listening incessantly to the raging of the world and I stand before myself as a second-class man. People may say what they want. It is a fact: someone who is young and healthy and does not fight at the decisive point is not someone I want to be. And yet I cannot leave – the devil take it! Probably I am also much too stupid to accomplish anything. … Our battles in the east and west are wonderful. I will never get over the fact that, in my entire life, I cannot take part in them. Damn!

In August 1917 the regiment finally received its marching orders and left Courland, crossed the Daugava river and took part in the conquest of Riga, which fell on 3 September. On 26 September he writes another letter to his little sister:

> Everything is under the sign of the vilest barbarism, as an advance coming to a sudden halt entails, with all its images of fire, destruction, emigration and so forth. I still have the hope that we come to a conclusion with Russia and this endless winter will not pass over us again like the year before when I nearly went crazy due to the lack of intellectual and physical exercise. How hard must this time be for prisoners and how immeasurably better we fare ourselves in comparison!

* * *

While Kurt von Plettenberg was on the Eastern Front, his father was in command of the Guard Corps until 1917. On the Western Front and later in Galicia he distinguished himself in many battles. 'For the heroic achievements of his units' during the war against France in September 1915 the emperor conferred on him the Pour le Mérite. 'Not I, but every single man at the front, deserved it', Karl von Plettenberg declared after the war. Yet in January 1917, to the great surprise of many, he tendered his resignation. Shortly before, the Chief of the Military Cabinet, General von Lyncker, had written to Plettenberg that the latter's superior, Crown Prince Rupprecht of Bavaria, had forced his retirement through. Emperor Wilhelm had not been able to take part in the discussion about this decision in the war cabinet. A little later he wrote personally to Karl von Plettenberg saying that the matter would have taken a different turn had he been there.

The official reason Lyncker gave him in a letter dated 17 January 1917 was that doubts had been expressed 'whether the long duration of the war and everything which you personally and the Guard Corps went through and accomplished did not after all impair your performance, and if you were equal to the great and difficult tasks which might be imminent in the very near future'. He added how difficult this decision had been for the emperor, but the latter could not have defied the judgement of Plettenberg's superior officers. Plettenberg could set the date of the resignation himself. Clara, his wife, wrote him a tender comforting letter from Berlin:

> You have achieved much, more than most people, and have accomplished something for the fatherland. It is certainly difficult to leave just now when new fierce battles lie ahead, difficult to be here at home without occupation. Yet for me the great comfort lies in the fact that you will return home to us, who love you and have been waiting longingly for your return for 130 weeks. It would have been better you had marched home as victor with your proud troops, but we shall resign ourselves to that which is given to us, even to this, my dear old heart, we will bear it together like so many things which have happened to us in the last 30 years.

Kurt was also heartbroken by this. How close his relationship to his father was can be gleaned from his letter to him dated 28 January 1917:

> My dear, dear father!
> Just now I have received your letter which of course saddened me deeply. … You write, so touchingly and without bitterness, that I am comforted for now, although I would like to cry incessantly. … I have always understood you, my dear papa, I know how much misfortune has befallen you during this war. … I wish I could be with you and tell you <u>how</u> much I love you.

Kurt's friend Axel von dem Bussche later learned from his father that Plettenberg could not reconcile himself to the policy of attrition and 'bleeding the enemy dry' practised since Verdun. He had argued that it would inevitably lead to slaughter, the destruction of decency and thus to the perdition of the individual soldier. In a letter to his wife Clara he had already written from the Western Front that he was quarrelling with his superiors almost daily. In conclusion Karl wrote on this matter in his memoirs:

> Whether I could have still achieved something extraordinary was naturally unpredictable; yet the emperor later wrote to me from Amerongen that the revolution undertaken with entirely inadequate means would not have achieved its goals so quickly, if Kessel or I had had the command in Berlin. At any rate it would have 'exploded' in Berlin.

The emperor confers on Plettenberg the Order of the Black Eagle as a farewell gift in January 1917, the highest Prussian decoration, and the Grand Cross of the Order of the Red Eagle. With the previous award of the Pour le Mérite, von Plettenberg was one of the few generals to receive the three highest honours of that period. In addition the emperor made him *Oberjägermeister* (Chief Master of the Hunt) shortly before the end of the war which, however, became redundant after the revolution of 1918. The Crown Prince expressed his esteem for the general in a personal letter of 11 May 1919: 'Of all my regiment commanders under whom I have served I have always valued Your Excellency the most. Your personal vigour, the dashing riding, the love for hunting, the warm human heart for your subordinates, and most of all your belief in the value of staunchness, discipline and punctuality were spoken from my heart, too. And all that I have learned from you in this respect, has become a guiding star for my entire military career thereafter.'

The October Revolution in Russia brought an armistice on the Eastern Front. After that IR 408 to which Kurt von Plettenberg belonged was redeployed to the Western Front. Until the end of the war in November 1918 he was assigned to the staff of the 1st Foot Guards led by Major Count Eulenburg. From a letter dated

January 1918 to Elisabeth von Sydow we learn that even at this stage he still believed in a 'victorious peace': 'The belief in a victorious end to the war is common and I rejoice at this every day. I for my part do not wish for anything but that I will at last participate in the great final battle of this war to which I was physically distant most of the time, yet intensively followed in my heart.

This wish would be fulfilled. Since he wrote only shortly before that he had had absolutely enough of war and shooting was highly unpleasant to him, these sentences are a surprise. Most repugnant to him was mainly the dreariness of positional warfare. In view of the possibility of proving himself, these statements seem to be simply wiped away.

There are no personal records of the last year of the war. It is certain that he participated in the last German offensive on the Western Front in summer 1918 and witnessed the further development of the war there. The Allies got the upper hand over the exhausted German forces, primarily with the aid of the massive military intervention of the Americans. Northern France and Belgium had to be evacuated, after the Allies succeeded on 8 August 1918 in breaking through at the Battle of Amiens. This begins their final offensive.

Quartermaster-General Erich Ludendorff later declared this defeat to be the 'blackest day of the German army'. A few days later the emperor and Ludendorff's government realised that the war could no longer be won by military means. Nevertheless the fighting continued.

It was hoped that defensive operations would paralyse the Allies' will to fight. The general pleads for greater discipline and repression to combat war-weariness on the home front. Germany should only offer peace negotiations after the next success in the West. In any case they want to keep the territorial gains in Eastern Europe.

The turning point arrived with Ludendorff's physical collapse at the end of September 1918 and the surrender of Bulgaria which could no longer resist the Allies. As the alliance of the Central Powers was critically weakened in south-eastern Europe, Ludendorff announced on behalf of the Supreme Army Command – which had been set above the emperor and political institutions and had made all the important decisions – Germany had to immediately request an armistice. For this purpose a government authorised by the parliament should be formed. By this step Ludendorff intended to pin the responsibility for the foreseeable defeat on the new government under Prince Max of Baden which the Social Democrats, the Centre Party and the Liberals had joined.

Actually it was less war-weariness on the home front and more the hopeless outlook at the Western Front which lead to this desperate appraisal of the situation. The wider public, however, knew little of these back-room agreements. Later the phrase 'undefeated in the field' was coined and circulated – the beginning of the 'stab in the back' myth.

On the night of 4 October 1918 the imperial government finally sent a note to the US President Woodrow Wilson asking him to bring about an immediate ceasefire and initiate peace negotiations on the basis of his Fourteen Points. The supreme army command deliberately stayed in the background and thus avoided any responsibility.

On 10th October 1918, when the end of war is already on the horizon, Kurt von Plettenberg's confidence in a 'victorious peace' had finally vanished. In a letter to Elisabeth the voice of their father seems to resonate: 'Naturally we are all very sad about the military events at the Western Front. Yet one thing is probably responsible for the events: the constant chatter of peace. Therefore, the boys all think that the war would end soon without them having their bones shot to pieces. The matter has now to be put in order somehow.' He cannot recognise the true causes of Germany's defeat at that time – like so many of his comrades. The propaganda of the supreme army command is too effective.

The young lieutenant remained with his regiment until 6 November 1918. Due to a dental abscess his commander sent him to Düsseldorf where to undergo proper medical treatment. A thief took advantage of his absence and stole all his possessions, among them diaries, clothes as well as his hunting rifle, an extraordinarily accurate weapon with two scopes. The outbreak of the revolution and the closure of the Rhine bridges made his return to his troops impossible. He left his regiment with the Iron Cross 1st and 2nd Class as well as the Knight's Cross with Swords of the Saxon Albrecht Order and the Medal of Merit of Schaumburg-Lippe. A few days later he showed up in borrowed civilian clothes at his family's home in Koslitz, Silesia.

If we consider Kurt von Plettenberg's statements in the preserved diaries and letters, the war which he joined with youthful enthusiasm took a rather disappointing course for him. He wanted to prove himself in combat, not least to his father, the imperial general. Beyond personal ambition and a thirst for adventure, this desire to acquit himself well arose to a large part from behaviour condition by social norms, also. Since childhood contempt for death, bravery and honour were been held up to him as values to aspire to. Although Kurt von Plettenberg chose a civilian career, the Prussian military attitude of the Wilhelmine Empire was natural to him. Likewise the duty to obey his superiors, which was religiously sanctioned especially in the Protestant milieu, was part of his conduct.

Therefore, acquitting himself well did not mean to take a stand for something arbitrarily, but to distinguish oneself in a predefined framework. In the sense of the chivalrous tradition, this meant the commitment of one's own life, a sacrifice which has to be made in the battle for that which is right. The ideal is fighting without fear, with the exultation to pursue a meaningful task greater than one's own insignificant existence.

He explained the events after the collapse of the front and revolutionary movements at home in terms of mass psychology. He wrote to his cousin Elisabeth:

Let's just say that the mass is like water, equally superficial, equally dependent in its movements on external impact. Should it be stirred, it creates waves, should it be heated, it boils up, and if the lid does not fit the pot, as which our old system may be seen, than it spoils over and throws down the lid. ... Please understand, I do not blame the people, because they were not ungrateful, but just dependent. And the agitators, yes, of course I am against these gentlemen or at least against three-quarters of them, and with nine out of ten of them I am angry with good reason. However, as with Napoleon, the victory of evil is the cowardice and laziness of the good. Everybody has his share of the blame.

His forgiving attitude towards 'the people' – and he does not dismiss them as 'riff-raff' as so many of his social class did – was probably the result of his experience of the community at the front, the experience of camaraderie beyond class boundaries. At any rate his war experiences enhance in Kurt von Plettenberg a character trait which later many of his friends and staff have noticed and valued in him, his highly developed sense of justice and his social empathy. Particularly because of this he was very popular with those who worked with and for him.

Yet the conservative pattern of thought can also be detected in Kurt von Plettenberg, which contrasted the elite with 'the masses', the ignorant, easily-led people. He could not perceive that much of the new-found autonomy of 'the people' is expressed in the strikes of the workers in the armament industry of 1917/18, the mutinies of the sailors, and the revolutionary battles of the workers. The fear of left-wing radicalisation, of a 'Sovietisation', which he shares with many contemporaries, blinds him.

Even years after the end of the First World War he explained the defeat in war and the subsequent revolution as the nefarious work of 'egoists' and 'troublemakers' who had betrayed the legacy of the 'best of all classes ' – it should be emphasised of *all* classes. He contrasted the war profiteers with the 'noble', the chivalrous people who have sacrificed their lives, and worried about the missed opportunity for a moral renewal of the people. In 1925 he wrote to Elisabeth von Sydow:

> Should we not think that if the greatest socialist of all times and nations – death – shows a people his lessons as plainly as the Germans, it would forget everything small and mean in the face of this immense socialisation? And now comes the question which was my starting point: Why did we not reach our goal, in particular why has everything which was done by the noble – and these were so many – been forgotten so quickly? There is actually only one explanation. Because we let it happen that while the best of all classes sacrificed their blood, weaklings and egoists of all kinds avoided this enormous experience of the nation and went their own way. And when the noble were used up by the superior power of the world branding against us year after year, then the troublemakers in the guise of saviours called the people's attention to the rabble not amenable to any great thought, and knowing this the people cannot be blamed much for the revolution. Today it is sad to see that 95 per cent business sense is almost everywhere valued higher than 95 per cent chivalry! Heroes are living in want, while racketeers are living the high life, only that it is even more surprising now after the great trial of the soul, for where does this development end, if we continue in this manner.

The satirical pictures of George Grosz or Otto Dix come to mind. The motif of the mislead people is also found in many other personal testimonies of noble officers, culminating in the 'legend of the stab in the back'. In 1923 General Hugo von Freytag-Loringhoven wrote in his autobiography:

> The army has gathered once more. It is a sad final battle which we were prevented from continuing by the revolution. … The duped German people, however, has been defrauded

of its good reputation by the imitation of Russian role models. The calamity which we did not manage to control in time took its course and swept away the imperial and all other German princely crowns.

Chapter 3

Difficult Years

At the beginning of November 1918 the sailors mutinied in Wilhelmshaven and Kiel because they refused to sail for a futile final battle against the British navy. In many cities workers' and soldiers' councils had been formed. After Kurt Eisner had proclaimed the Free State of Bavaria in Munich and the revolutionary movement had also taken hold in Berlin, Prince Max of Baden, as acting imperial chancellor, announced the abdication of the emperor on 9 November 1918 and conferred the office of imperial chancellor on Friedrich Ebert of the Social Democrats, the leader of the largest party in the Reichstag. On the afternoon of the same day, the Social Democrat Philipp Scheidemann had declared the 'German Republic' from a window of the Reichstag, while shortly after Karl Liebknecht proclaimed the 'Socialist Republic' from the back of a truck in front of the Berlin City Castle. The abdication of the German regional princes followed. The emperor was urged, against his will, to go into exile in Holland and the Crown Prince followed his example.

The Secretary of State, Matthias Erzberger of the Centre Party, had already been conducting ceasefire negotiations with the Allies since 7 November in the forest of Compiègne. The outcome was the Treaty of Versailles signed by the government on 28 June 1919. Alsace-Lorraine had to be vacated. All heavy weapons and armaments had to be handed in. Germany pledged itself to pay reparations to compensate for the damage suffered by the civilian populations of the Allied nations during the war.

The majority of the German people regarded the Treaty of Versailles as a 'disgraceful diktat'. The crippling level of reparations was a critical factor in the spread of revanchist sentiments, which were exploited by the nationalist parties in their campaign against the Weimar Republic.

The order to abandon their positions, which had been held until the Armistice despite increasing problems with discipline, came as a shock to many front-line officers. They knew nothing of the complete exhaustion of reserves which had caused Ludendorff to suggest to the emperor that negotiations begin in September 1918. After four years at the front – 'undefeated in the field' – most of them found the revolution incomprehensible. Their return home was a traumatic event.

The world of the nobility had collapsed with the fall of the monarchy. The end of the familiar order of things after the defeat was perceived as a complete disaster. The flight of the emperor, the central point of aristocratic society, was a fundamental break in their entire political orientation, especially for the older generation. Of course, as well as the defeat, many aristocratic families were also mourning fallen sons and fathers.

The nobility was also hit hard by the attack upon its leading role in state and society, the most obvious sign of which was the abolition of their titles, until now protected by the state, in the new Republican Constitution. The declaration that entailed estates would be abolished, by which means aristocratic landed property had been declared inalienable and indivisible so that it could be passed on undiminished to a single family member, weakened this social class further. To this was added the dramatically reduced prospects of their younger sons thanks to the reduction in the size of the officer corps, especially in Prussia. Due to the restrictions laid down by the Allies, only 862 of the more than 10,000 aristocratic officers who had served in the war and survived it were kept on active duty for the rebuilding of the armed forces of the Weimar Republic. The army now had a mere 4,000 officers. The rest of the aristocratic officers were 'off duty' between 1918 and 1920. Many aristocratic sons thus had no means of support.

After a short 'period of numbness', the nobility developed two strategies in an attempt to win back their position in state and society. The first was the use of force, as in the counter-revolutionary actions of the Freikorps such as the Ehrhardt Brigade. They wanted to overthrow the Republic, and were responsible for the murders of Rosa Luxemburg and Karl Liebknecht. It was a futile attempt to turn time back by force. The second, and more successful, strategy was the formation of special-interest groups which from then on pursued aggressive lobbying.

Among them was first and foremost the *Adelsgenossenschaft* (Association of the Nobility), founded in 1874, which had a considerable increase in membership at this time, particularly from the minor gentry. The wealthier nobles, who still owned large estates, gathered in knightly orders and 'gentlemen's clubs'. As well as these two tendencies, however, there also existed a kind of 'escapism', a renunciation of politics, a retreat to their country homes, which was linked to an attitude of wait-and-see and of restraint.

* * *

The war ended for Kurt von Plettenberg with his return to his parents and sister at Koslitz in Silesia, where the father had rented a small castle with hunting grounds. Yet the internal political struggles following the end of the war did not leave him untouched. However, he neither joined the Freikorps nor was he active in the Adelsgenossenschaft. He experienced the fall of the Hohenzollern family, the abdication of the supreme commander and the federal princes and the flight of the emperor to Holland equally as far-reaching events, but violent reaction was alien to his nature. The radical change in society in which his family had held a privileged position unsettled him. 'Believe me that all this has affected me much more than the war', he wrote in a letter to his sister Luise in January 1919.

Von Plettenberg was 27 years old at the end of the war. As early as December 1918, only a month after his demobilisation, he resumed his studies. He attended the still-obligatory law lectures and then enlarged upon his knowledge of forestry during an intermittent semester at the University of Munich. Here, at the Faculty of Forestry, he found lifelong friends in Albrecht Duke of Bavaria and the later famous aviator Wolf Baron von Stutterheim.

Apart from these contacts, student life in Munich was not easy for him. As a retired imperial general, his father was unable support his son in a manner befitting his class during this time. Already of barely-sufficient means, unfortunately he lost the rest of his possession when his apartment in Munich caught fire. Elisabeth von Sydow wrote of him in her memoirs: 'He was hungry and cold during his university years, as it is the case after a lost war.' But with his optimistic nature the future forestry official looked forward and relies upon his active spirit. The study of forestry keeps him from losing his social position. The network of old family ties is certainly helpful, too.

Yet the situation in Munich became problematic for young aristocrats, after Count Arco assassinated the Bavarian Minister-President Kurt Eisner on 21 February 1919. In order to be able to complete his studies as quickly and safely as possible, in mid-April von Plettenberg transferred to the Academy of Forestry in Eberswalde. There he can focus on preparing for taking his articles. Nevertheless, he follows the daily events with active interest. In particular, the arguments about the obligations of the Treaty of Versailles find a lively echo in his diary:

> And the peace of today? Never have more disgraceful conditions been offered to a people. Yet – regret comes too late. … We will be enslaved like no other people before us. The National Assembly is outraged. Now they have finally realised that our enemies were serious about this! What may come? … While the fatherland fares in shame and disgrace, we are kept in suspense by the ridiculous exam. … The extradition [of the emperor to the Allies, which was in fact not carried out] has

been signed, too, such a shameful peace has probably never been made as long as the world has existed.

On 27 June 1919 he passed the First State Examination as one of the best in his year. At the beginning of his two-year trainee clerkship, in July 1919 the ministry sent him to the remote forest district of Rothebude in the Gumbinnen region of East Prussia, to cover for a forester who was seriously ill. He had no-one to introduce him to the unfamiliar demands of his post. Entirely on his own, he battled bureaucratic demands which forced him to stay at his desk for most of the day. In his diary he lamented the 'lost time' during which he believed that he was learning nothing. To make matters worse, his stay in Rothebude was extended by the ministry by another six months.

The young forester had no choice but to concentrate on his work, especially when the previous forester died. Occasional visits by friends and the councillor of forestry, who comes periodically to check the accounts, bring some relief from his great solitude in joint hunting trips. It is the East Prussian landscape which stabilises and strengthens his soul. Again and again, similar to his time on the Eastern Front, it is the magnificent experience of landscape, the forests teeming with deer and the lakes at the turn of the seasons, which delight him and help him to cope with the loneliness.

When von Plettenberg could finally leave Rothebude in summer 1920, he was overjoyed, especially after the forestry councillor praised him highly for his work in front of the assembled company during his farewell party. Also in Gumbinnen – far from the unrest – he followed current political developments with great attention. This would not change in the years to come. The fate of his 'poor fatherland' endlessly preoccupied him. It satisfied him immensely that the Dutch refused to extradite the emperor whom the Allies wished to put on trial as a war criminal. On 26 January 1920 he noted: 'Holland's splendid answer! There are finally still some decent people in the world. How could one rejoice, if only one's own homeland would find such forceful language again. I won't forget the Dutch for this all my life.'

In March 1920 the abortive Kapp Putsch took place. The putschists wanted to topple the government and restore the previous regime. Plettenberg appeared to be surprised: 'Kapp and Lüttwitz made complete fools of themselves. It looks gloomy on the political horizon now.' And it does not brighten up for him in the following months. On 22 January 1922 he noted: 'In the evening German national meeting; not very productive. I am moving closer to Stresemann all the time.' He very much regretted the latter's early death in 1929.

In general, it is clear that von Plettenberg judged politicians more on their personality than on their party affiliations, so he was happy that the Christian Centre Party's Adam Stegerwald, chairman of the Christian Federation of Trade Unions, was elected Minister-President of Prussia as he considered him to be a man above party politics.

He was very critical of the political intrigues and the party squabbles of the Weimar Republic. Nevertheless he increasing came more into line with the position of the Social Democrats. When the Social Democratic party conference in Görlitz opted for a coalition of the centre, he greeted this with the words: 'The pinkos as a party supportive of the state; we are approaching Stegerwald's ideal which is also mine!!' And when the Prussian government was formed in the autumn, his diary reads: 'Otto Braun as Minister-President and Severing as Minister of the Interior – two of the best brains of the left!'

His reaction to the murder of government ministers by fanatical nationalists show how far he had moved away from that kind of thinking. The assassination of Matthias Erzberger, vilified as an 'appeasement politician' in August 1921 by the Freikorps, he commented with the words: 'Signs of stormy weather! It is an outrageous deed which can only be damaging. Hopefully the guilty will at least be caught.' Walter Rathenau's assassination by the same types in June 1922 he called: 'Crime and madness'.

His original monarchist attitudes were no longer unshaken, either. He took a critical view of the exiled emperor, deploring his rash remarrying only one year after the death of Empress Auguste Viktoria to the widowed Princess Hermine von Schönaich-Carolath, 28 years his junior, as a 'public immoral act', and on the 'Emperor's birthday' on 27 January he vehemently noted in his diary that the abdicated emperor 'has destroyed the 500-year-old glory of the house of Hohenzollern by utter failure!!' Plettenberg's trust in the paternal competence and benevolence of the emperor, which had still been discernible in a letter from the front on 8 May 1915 to his fifteen-year-old sister, had been shaken.

In the years that followed Kurt von Plettenberg made few comments about the House of Hohenzollern and on the form of government. Yet he lived quite naturally with the Prussian-Hohenzollern tradition. Encouraged by his family's history, he is close to the imperial family, but it cannot be assumed posthumously whether he supported the reintroduction of the monarchy or a constitutional monarchy. Marion Dönhoff said later that he was not a monarchist. Yet he knew the imperial family very well and felt connected to them on a personal level, as his father had been. For the sake of family ties, not political reasons, Plettenberg supported the Hohenzollern family.

The political development of the Weimar Republic also concerned him in the following years. Normally optimistic, he appeared to have become resigned to the situation. After a rally against the occupation of the Ruhr in January 1923 he noted: 'Actually all that left me cold. It sometimes feels as if the revolution has shattered all my enthusiasm.' He commented on the Hitler-Ludendorff putsch of 1923 as follows:

> It is highly deplorable that great generals take to the streets in the manner of Communists. We need something other than coups. A real personage is necessary. A man who 'drives the moneylenders from the temple', who can wield the sword of judgement without fear of the people, who is our, the German

people's, guide to old German tradition and to new strong
belief.

The longing for a powerful personality also comes through, for a
leader of strong character who would be able to be a guide out of
the miserable situation. Many of his generation and social class
yearn for a political leadership embodying authority and doing
justice to the fatherland, because to their experience of instability
and change in the post-war period. Yet at that moment he did not
see such qualities in either Ludendorff or Hitler.

By the beginning of 1921 Kurt von Plettenberg had enrolled at
the academy of forestry in Hannoversch-Münden in order to
prepare for the Second State Examination. After an intensive
period of study, he passed in Berlin in May 1921 with good
grades. Only two fellow students were placed higher than him.
He could then finally take up his first post. He chose public
service and would have preferred to go to Liegnitz where he
would be close to his parents. However, the administration sent
him to Stralsund. In May 1921 he started work as head of
department for the timber trade at the Stralsund government. To
his chagrin, as in Rothebude in East Prussia, he is entirely on his
own and complains that he has nobody to introduce him to the
customs of the area. It took him some time to get to grips with
this entirely unfamiliar job.

Furthermore he is fed up with his bachelor existence. He
writes to his sister: 'I actually would really like to marry. But
whom? I liked Anni "a lot", but not "in that way".' His
relationship with her, whom he had met in Stralsund, did not
develop in the way the now thirty-year-old wanted. He blamed
himself and thought that his rashness had disappointed her
deeply. He spent his free time reading, primarily historical-
political and philosophical works, but also classical literature. He
went to the cinema and visited the theatre. Occasionally he was
invited to hunting parties in the surrounding area or visited
friends and family, as far as his means allowed it. Valued and
respected by his friends, he nevertheless lamented his loneliness

again and again in his diary. His emotional support in these years came only from Elisabeth, his 'dear cousin'. He later thanks her for her belief in his abilities at a time when he still had not found his inner balance.

> <u>What</u> an effect you have had on me, you probably do not know yourself. Yet I had been forcibly sidelined for too long during the war and thus had really lost joy in myself. ... By showing me trust ... and treating me as if I was really worth something and as if I could become someone decent, you awoke in me a certain self-confidence and now perhaps it will even develop further.

His low spirits improved when he met Heinrich Count Dönhoff. On the latter's invitation, in June 1922 Plettenberg visited Friedrichstein Castle near Königsberg for the first time. The count's extensive forests and the house impressed him. Heinrich Count Dönhoff, some years younger than him, who managed the estate, pleased him 'as much as only few people before'. Apparently a possible future for Kurt von Plettenberg in Friedrichstein had already been discussed on that occasion. For in his diary there is this confession: 'I am almost sad that I feel duty-bound to remain faithful to public service in these grim times, since I would have probably enjoyed my work more in Friedrichstein.'

It would take more than half a year until he decided in February 1923, having meanwhile been promoted to senior forestry official, to accept the offer from Friedrichstein to manage the large forests of the family there. Two matters made him hesitate: firstly, the future of the big landowners was still uncertain. Secondly, he also 'slightly fears the personal dependency'. The balance is finally tipped by the fact that he no longer enjoys office work and is furthermore impeded by political interference. In retrospect he spoke of the fact, 'that I had to learn in Stralsund how district presidents and governors of social democratic and democratic leanings interfered in the affairs of the officials of the forest administration in an unobjective and sometimes even improper manner. The late head forester Barth, but especially I, have had to suffer from these circumstances at that time, which were also the cause for several reports sent to Berlin.'

From now on, the young senior forest official consistently took the road of self-discipline and study. Nobody had to instruct him any longer. Even if he asked himself again and again over these years in an almost self-tormenting manner whether he meets the expectations set by himself, he never mourned for the past. Intellectual freedom is his goal and this is based on self-improvement, in his view. Tirelessly he completed his education, as the reading lists in his diary show. To train his brain he occasionally wrote in his diary with his left hand, although he usually used the right, and learnt pieces of classical literature by heart. He also liked to read aloud on evenings in company.

However, a meaningful life was not only tied to spirit and thoughts in Plettenberg's opinion. A zest for and enjoyment of life were part of it too. As in his youth, his studies with friends and family, and during military service he enjoyed company and values discussions. All his friends emphasise his humour. And he loved smoking; there is hardly a picture of him without a cigarette. Influenced by his wartime experiences and also by the period of solitude he developed in these years which will become so characteristic for him: internal freedom. In one of the many volumes by Christian Morgenstern he found a poem which corresponds to his understanding of himself:

> Freedom is no dish one can buy;
> You have it or you have it not.
> And whoever has real freedom,
> could include a little smile.

Chapter 4

Marion Countess Dönhoff

The yellow buttercups were in flower along the banks of the Pregola and on the ample meadows 'the bluish pink of the cuckoo flowers [was] intermingled with the high grass', when Kurt von Plettenberg arrived from Stralsund at the Dönhoffs' Friedrichstein Castle in East Prussia. Presumably he drove along the ancient alley of elm trees which leads from Löwenhagen to Friedrichstein, then down the sunken road and on the left caught sight of the lake, and on the right the magnificent view of the castle.

Plettenberg is received 'charmingly' in Friedrichstein, as his first diary entry there reads. Probably the family had tea with him on the terrace or in the garden room from where there was a wide view of the park with its alleys down to the Pregola meadows. Countess Maria was still in the house; she only moved a year later to Barthen, her widow's house, for Count August Karl Dönhoff had died in 1920. His youngest daughter Marion, eleven years old at the time of his death, moved there with her. During the first days Heinrich Dönhoff shows Plettenberg the estate and they make day trips to Crantz and to the ornithological station at Rossitten. Then the management of Dönhoff's forests begins.

At first the castle's former courtroom is portioned off as a separate apartment for the senior forester. In July 1924 he changes quarters and moves into the old forestry office in Löwenhagen where he is independent: 'My apartment is furnished quite nicely and has become very cosy', he wrote in his diary in July 1924. 'H. Dönhoff is charming to me. In general I like the people here very

47

much. It is a shame that we need so much sleep. I would love to be able to work 20 hours.' His life there was especially comfortable, since his favourite cousin Elisabeth von Sydow visits him for several months on several occasions to manage his household and to take care of the garden. He was grateful to her. 'She adds sparkle to my winter', he wrote in 1925 and recalls fondly their evenings spent harmoniously reading together.

Plettenberg felt accepted in East Prussia. This feeling can be understood if the description of the development of a large agricultural estate using the example of the family seat in Marion Dönhoff's doctoral thesis is considered. At that time in the East the owners managed their own estates, 'they were virtually entrepreneurs, while in the west the large estates were leased to small farmers' and 'the owner merely acted as a rent collector ... Therefore it is not surprising that the relationship between owners and subordinates was very different; in the east more paternalistic, if you like more servile, yet also closer and more cordial than in the West. People depended more on each other; in addition in each generation upstairs and downstairs knew each other pretty well, which resulted in a peculiar mix of institutional distance and personal familiarity.'

Originally from Westphalia, the Dönhoffs had moved to Livonia in the fourteenth century with the Teutonic Knights and had settled in East Prussia at the beginning of the seventeenth century. In 1633 they had been made imperial counts by the emperor in Vienna. On the River Pregola, not far from Königsberg, they bought the basic stock of the Friedrichstein estate and extended the property during the next hundred years. At the beginning of the eighteenth century they built the baroque castle, one of the most beautiful in East Prussia. The great palace façade at the garden front gave the impression of a royal seat. In the course of the centuries many crowned heads had been guests, among them Friedrich Wilhelm I.

Pestilence and war had caused numerous major setbacks for the estate's owners, but the property was secured in the nineteenth century and the debts paid off. August Heinrich Count

Dönhoff had turned the property into an entailed estate in 1859, by which means the heir was from then on merely an owner on trust and had to provide for or pay out to those who did not inherit. With this, the break-up of the estate by inheritance was prevented.

From 1923 to 1930 von Plettenberg was responsible for the management of the Dönhoffs' extensive forests: he selected the timber to be cut and organised its sale. He took care of the planting of trees, designed plans for the maintenance and protection of the forest areas and assigned the forest workers. To this had to be added extensive correspondence and the accounts. The forest property, besides agriculture, was the estate's most important source of income. As representative of Count Dönhoff he, the trained forester, would also work in the non-forestry departments of the large administration.

At the beginning of his job it was not easy for him to make a profit. Especially in the first year, at the beginning of 1923, when rampant inflation drove up the dollar rate to which all payments were linked, management must have been difficult. Sometimes the dedicated forester still managed, as he noted with satisfaction, to sell the timber before the next price drop.

The German economy improved only slowly in the next few years. Inflation was addressed with the consolidation of the currency at the end of 1923, while the Dawes and Young Plans reduced the burden of reparations and the economy was able to recover. Relations between Germany and France improved and the occupation of the Ruhr ended, ushering in a brief phase of political and economic stability, lasting until the Great Depression in 1928. The estate owners east of the Elbe benefitted from this. The sale of venison made up only a small part of the proceeds from the forest, but naturally gamekeeping and hunting were among the tasks of the forest manager. In his diaries Kurt Plettenberg kept a careful account of the many hunting forays and his kills.

After a period of adjustment he was successfully managing the extensive forests, although he himself frequently noted in his diary that he still had a lot to learn and did not entirely meet the requirements of the responsibility given to him yet. He even cut his own salary in 1926 'without asking Heini, since for now my work is not worth more'. Demanding the highest standards of himself not only professionally, but also personally, was typical of him. He could not be satisfied with mediocrity and thus emphasised again and again his inadequacy, as he perceived it. His former regimental commander, Count Eulenburg, defined this characteristic of high personal standards rather as self-underestimating and mildly criticised it. Immediately after the war he had written to von Plettenberg:

> You have the same 'fault of your merits' as our dear Karl Wilhelm: you underestimate yourself. You have meant much to me not just personally, but also in your service. You were anything but 'useless as M.G.O.' [machine gun officer]. I also don't know who I could have found lacking in 'initiative and vigour' less than you. On the contrary, these traits in particular made your services so valuable to me.

Marion Dönhoff, later reading some excerpts of Plettenberg's diaries, took also note of his self-criticism with some surprise. She wrote to Plettenberg's son after the war:

> I was not aware of this at all, and only based on these notes I realised that he also had a melancholy side full of self-doubt. We – my siblings and I – had laughed so much together with him, ridden together, hunted and discussed – despite some worries – that we actually only knew his sunny side.

Evidently he was very capable of hiding these doubts even from his friends. To this is added that in these circles people were obliged to hide their feeling and be disciplined, and the 'minor key' was not taken notice of in oneself or others.

'I have hardly known anyone else so filled with inner serenity', Marion Dönhoff remembered. His humour was legendary, as he was able 'to discern and articulate the funny side of situations and the amusing aspect of small human weaknesses with unerring accuracy'. That he was constantly optimistic and cheerful in the company of others was certainly decisive for his popularity: 'Yes, he had become so much a part of us', wrote Marion Dönhoff in a letter to his widow, 'that somebody once said that of the Dönhoffs Plettenberg is actually the nicest.'

Alexander Prince zu Dohna-Schlobitten described the eight-years-older man in his *Memoirs of an Old East Prussian* as follows:

> Kurt Plettenberg ... was one of the most unusual people I knew ... Kurt Plettenberg was a role model to me: personally, politically, and also in his economic views. He was among the very few people whose picture I always carry with me in a kind of internal gallery, and I thank God that this extraordinary man crossed my path.

Furthermore Plettenberg was a very sociable person who knew how to entertain those around him. So he loved to recite poems which he learned by heart whilst shaving in the morning, ballads by Uhland, Goethe's poems and also funny ones by Ringelnatz and Morgenstern. 'Therefore he was called', as Marion Dönhoff recalls, 'Chief Shooting Anthropoid' (Opupa), based on Morgenstern whom we venerated – all of us loved him and admired his all-round nature and erudition.' The nickname alludes to Plettenberg's love of hunting and is taken from the poem 'Anto-logy' from the 'Gallows Songs' by Christian Morgenstern.

> Of yore, on earth was dominant
> the biggest mammal: the gig-ant
>
> ('Gig' is a numeral so vast,
> it's been extinct for ages past)
>
> But off, like smoke, this vastness flew.

51

Time did abound, and numbers too,

Until one day a tiny thing,
the Tweleph-ant, was chosen king.

Where is he now? Where is his throne?
In the museum pales his bone.
True, Mother Nature gave with grace
the Eleph-ant us in his place,

but, woe, that shooting anthropoid
called 'Man ', in quest for tusks destroyed

him ere he could degenerate,
by stages to Ten-ant's state.

O noble club, SPCA,
Don't let Man wholly take away

The steps of that titanic scale
That leads still farther down the trail.

How grateful will the Ant survive
If left to flourish and to thrive,

Until he, in a far-off year,
As Zero-ant will disappear.

Despite this familiarity with the Dönhoffs there were of course differences, regarding the business side. More and more Plettenberg not only managed the forests by himself, but also the entire entailed estate, as the young count is often absent. Marion Dönhoff later writes: 'For a long time Heini could not get used to having to be present at all times. The sense of responsibility and enjoyment of leadership only developed in his late twenties.' Heinrich Dönhoff's passion is mainly for the theatre and the exciting cultural milieu of 1920s Berlin. In addition he works optimistically with modern methods, which made the cautious Plettenberg uneasy, who found the emerging credit service in the agricultural sector dubious: 'Count Heini is still charming, but too enthusiastic in large-scale business operations', his diary of autumn 1924 read.

Plettenberg's health was also causing him problems in these years. Out in the forest he had caught a chronic kidney disease in the wet and cold winter of 1924. 'From New Year till 22nd February quiet times; a miserable winter for me, difficult in terms of forestry, as only little timber can be transported in the squashy January weather and I myself constantly wade through the mud!' He often felt exhausted. He took a cure at Karlsbad to regenerate for work, but noticed that it brought hardly any improvement. Furthermore, he badly bruised his face when he collided with a tree branch at full gallop. It required two painful operations on his nose, the first being unsuccessful as breathing difficulties continued.

Regardless of his professional and health problems, Plettenberg travelled a lot. He did not just follow the political developments of those years from afar, hidden away in the forest. He went to veterans' reunions in Berlin and Potsdam to meet old comrades and university friends, to Bavaria to meet his friend Duke Albrecht, to his parents in Silesia and to his old Westphalian homes in Himmighusen, Westhusen and Sandfort.

In 1929 he decided to leave Friedrichstein, although his appointment was for life. He took over the direction of the forestry department in the main administration of the chamber of agriculture for the province of Brandenburg and Berlin. It is unclear what made him re-enter public service which he had left with such relief in Stralsund in 1923. For almost at the same time he received an offer from the court chamber of the House of Hohenzollern to take over the forestry department there. The court chamber controlled eight forest districts and the Cadinen estate. The salary would have corresponded to that of a public head forester, and at the same time the office would have entailed being deputy to the president. Plettenberg declines because he feels obliged to honour his pledge to Berlin. Later the president of the court chamber von Garnier writes to him:

> I have just received your courteous letter of the 3rd of this month and can only say that its contents are quite suited to spoil my day today. I had already heard rumours that the chamber of agriculture is interested in you, yet still believed to forestall them, and now I find out to my chagrin that I have come too late by one postal day. That you were spared the agony of choice for now, I appreciate on your behalf. Alas, it is of no avail to me.

Clearly Plettenberg was now valued as a forestry and administrative expert beyond the circle of East Prussian landowners. Here again his fidelity to principles becomes evident. He stands by his commitment, even if the other offer is perhaps more attractive.

So he left East Prussia. It might have been the case that something very private was the decisive factor, linked to his desire to marry: his friendship with Marion Dönhoff. She herself published nothing in her memoirs of her childhood and her East Prussian homeland about her relationship with Kurt von Plettenberg in those years. She wrote in 1982 that she had a bit of a guilty conscience regarding this, yet 'it was simply too difficult'. She stood by her maxim: 'Private matters have to remain private.' An exception to this was in *Memories of Kurt Baron von Plettenberg*, written in 1985 on the occasion of a commemorative event in Bückeburg. It states therein:

> That somebody who was 20 years older than me, who could tell of important people and distant regions, knew innumerable poems by heart – not only serious ones by Goethe, but also funny ones by Morgenstern and Ringelnatz – that such a man was willing to make serious conversation with me, was an experience I marvelled at time and again.

Key to the understanding of their great friendship, however, as it may be presumed, is the 'great water accident'. On 3 August 1924 the Dönhoffs undertook a trip to the Baltic Sea to Cranz. They took two cars. In one of them were the adults, in the other six children and a driver who was unfamiliar with the surroundings. Marion was accompanied by her cousin Huberta Kanitz, little Franz Coudenhove from Austria and his sister as well as two Lindemann siblings from Switzerland. In the evening they travelled back to Friedrichstein at dusk. Marion Dönhoff recalled:

> In Königsberg a thunderstorm broke out, and the rain impeded visibility. We children … were singing and fooling about in the car, when suddenly the driver emitted a terrible cry. At the same moment the car seemed to plunge into a construction pit, but then an enormous deluge of water rushed in on us: the Pregola, this thought shot through my head.
>
> It was not an entirely closed car; it had a so-called American canvas top. Immediately, wild chaos erupted inside the car. As the driver later stated, he was driven to the back by the vortex, everything whirled about. Then there was a jolt: apparently the car touched the river bottom, ten metres deep at that spot: I had run out of air long ago and continued to gulp water.
>
> It is unbelievable how fast the thoughts rush through one's head in the face of death. I had to think how stupid people are who say that drowning is a quick death. My God, how long it took. I pictured how sad it is for those remaining behind, when six children are laid in the hall next to each other. Then suddenly a last thought flashed through my head: there was a gap between car body and top. I felt around, searched for it, pushed myself through and was yanked upwards. An eternity passed.
>
> Finally at the surface, I saw the spotlights of car pushed onto the quay, and heard my name being called. Without my brother's call I would have gone under again, since all

strength had been spent; only dizziness remained. Yet with this I pulled myself together and paddled like a dog to the quay where long coats were lowered down. A final supreme effort was necessary to cling to the coat while those above pulled until the three meters to the road had been negotiated. I was the last emerging alive – after approximately five minutes, as my brother said. The two weakest, Huberta Kanitz and twelve-year-old Franz Coudenhove, were only to be recovered dead, hours later. Young Lindemann, who apparently had emerged, first dived in once more to rescue Coudenhove's sister. Finally I emerged last.

In Kurt Plettenberg's diary the following entry is found a day later:

4th August 1924: ... on 3rd August the most terrible car accident in Königsberg to which two lovely children and almost five other people fell victim. I was more upset than ever during the war. If I had only been there, maybe everything would have taken a different turn! It is too sad. ... I bring back Marion to Barthen at night. Then a number of restless days, the funeral service, many guests etc.

Marion herself wrote to Plettenberg's son half a century after this accident: 'On the drive back to my mother in Barthen to give her the sad news your dear father accompanied and comforted me, an entirely unforgotten deed.' Yet she does not speak of the time afterwards.

Plettenberg's entry of 4 August continues: 'Many beautiful, indeed most beautiful moonlit nights. The car accident had an epilogue for me – a peculiar one and yet most beautiful.' In this half-hour of comfort, for the drive from Friedrichstein to Barthen took this long, and during the moonlit walks in the days that followed the great and lasting affection and trust between the two was formed, which for many years remained alive and precious in both memories as an 'old friendship'.

What 'Opupa' meant to 'little Marion' in her years as a teenage girl, can be better understood, if her experiences as a child of her father, the Prussian chamberlain August Count Dönhoff, member of parliament and of the Prussian House of Lords, are taken into account:

> My most lasting impression of him is that given on many winter evenings. His study was the last in a long flight of rooms taking up the entire length of the park-side wing of the castle, measuring roughly 90 metres. Since all the doors always stood open, he could be seen at a great distance sitting at his desk illuminated by a lamp. It was as if one noticed a bright spot at the end of a long, dark tunnel. When I saw him somewhere during the day wandering through the house, I quickly sneaked away for fear of having to read to him. His eyesight was very bad … It was virtually torture if I did not manage to escape once in a while and I then had to muddle through texts completely incomprehensible to me.

Plettenberg, in contrast, is associated with the park, forests, meadows and fields, they ride, go camping or canoeing – often with her siblings and the Lehndorffs, or with guests – and 'he explains the world to her'. They also go hunting together, have discussions, philosophise, laugh, dance and enjoy life.

'The manner of interaction was different from today. People tended each other like gardens and were attentive', says Marion and she wrote to him years after his time in Friedrichstein:

> Actually it has been you who has influenced my life and my development, because it was you who taught me for the first time to view the world through your love and friendship and to admire it in its diversity.
>
> And you know yourself how receptive and impressionable one is at this age (I was only 14 years old when I met you!) – I believe that at that time there was hardly a thought, an idea or a set of issues not carrying

something of your nature and linking me to you, as it still does today.

For many years I have kept a little dog rose you gave me, which we once plucked together during a walk in Friedrichstein, and which resides with a letter, now a little yellow and brittle, - and because I wanted to send you a little flower conveying all my wishes to you, thus I have plucked this little rose recently at the blue Mediterranean coast, there where it is the most beautiful. ...

In old friendship faithfully and as always
Your Marion

Furthermore she later (1995) explained to Plettenberg's daughter: 'He was my first great love. Yet I did not want to commit myself yet at 17, 18', and wrote to her that same year:

My relationship to him never actually changed. – That our friendship did not end in marriage was simply due to the fact that I wanted to be free to build my own life, and because it became suddenly clear to me that he – who was twenty years older – had to be free for other decisions, therefore one day I wrote him a kind of farewell letter. If I still had his response which was so understanding and confident I would send it to you – but it remained in East Prussia.

However, his farewell letter was actually found in her papers in the archive of Crottof Castle:

Löwenhagen, 15 September 1928
My dear Marion,

A thousand thanks for your kind letter which I only received today on my return from holiday. I came home later than intended, as I needed to visit my parents. My little sister is ill and her condition is such no one can predict whether a happy outcome is possible. For us all it would be very sad; for my mother who buried three sons and three younger brothers, it would be terrible, if indeed the little one does not recover. My sister herself is fully aware of the situation and is of a harrowing calmness and kindness. She looked like a little saint and at her bedside I could very much sense the existence of something which transcends all reason. I will let you know soon again how everything turns out.

And now to your letter. In advance I would like to say that I understood all your thoughts completely. My dear little Marion, if I would not think about marriage in the same way as you, I would have probably tied the knot with someone long before I got to know you. All the outward paraphernalia of a wedding are an anathema to me, and to create an actually irreversible, as you so rightly put it, state which all people are watching constantly for a thousand different reasons is a terrible notion to me – as it is to you. Despite this, I have reached an inner acceptance of all these difficulties. I see no other possibility to order the cohabitation of people also for the general society than by a marriage sanctioned by the state; I cannot recognize what would give me the right to demand an exception for myself; in short I have to comply with the requirements of public opinion, simply because I know that only <u>much</u> greater men than me may infringe this famous order without great discomfort.

And as for <u>our</u> case: well, I will be honest with you, the reasons I named as obstacles were only pretences and I want to ask you to forgive me for daring to mention them. No, I have to say it openly, I knew <u>your</u> reasons – instinctively – and I respect and honour them, even if they represent the obstacles to the fulfilment of my former dreams and of plans you probably also once considered. Perhaps this sentiment driving you now to maintain your complete freedom for the next years represents much of the best in you. I really believe this – You will probably marry later. That will be something different to a certain extent. – And what shall I say in the end? If at my age a goal becomes unattainable after such long wanderings, it is no small matter. I have known this since – a long time, much longer than I wanted to admit to myself, because all of this emerged following the pattern of your development. And this development was such that it was long clear to me that the outcome would be the one we are now finally discussing openly. However, your development was not such that we have been estranged from each other in the slightest. That is the peculiar thing. You are as close to my heart today as in the last five years, - please forgive the triviality, but it is not just my imagination – when you enter the room, my heart misses a beat! We will <u>never</u> become strangers. Perhaps we even pass up something especially great. Yet even this is subject to the law of our progress through life – 'As on that day ...', says the old master!

And if you believe that I have helped you, and had influenced your development! Actually, this old goat – forgive me – would like to reverse this. I probably experienced <u>much</u> more joy and beauty in my life through you than vice versa.

So, little Marion! This letter marks the serious end of an era in our two lives. And if my heart would have written certain passages differently, reason dictates that the letter should be written as it appears here. This is also for <u>my own</u> good! You have filled my life in these last years with indescribable happiness and joy and for this I would like to thank you with all my heart. I accept your offer of friendship. And I will keep it, this promise I want to give to you, and you know already without further affirmation, how certain you can be of my loyalty.

In faithful old and new friendship

Yours Kurt Plettenberg

Both maintained the 'old and new' friendship. Marion Dönhoff wrote to Plettenberg's wife Arianne on 2 December 1976: 'To me he meant a lot, as you know and as it is clear from my letter, which was dated June 1944, as if it had been written in premonition of the final farewell.'

In the last letter from Marion Dönhoff to Kurt von Plettenberg it says:

11th June 1944

Opupa – very dearest, how happy your letter made me, my eternally faithful friend! Just recently you were so immensely kind, indeed, you cannot know how often I have this thought in deepest gratitude: How nice to have Opupa! . . . That which you touch upon in your letter and of which we spoke recently during our walk, is however not correct – never, not once in all those long years of our friendship there was the shadow or cloud in my heart, when I thought of you. Look, since the time that my 14-year-old heart beat faster for the first time, it was for a long, long time your image living inside it, first venerated and admired, then loved with the whole intensity and willingness of youth – yet always, even later, it was also touchstone and guideline and with this actually defining for my entire life, because it has shaped the idea I have of humanity in a decisive manner. Yet is it not actually much better to think that the notion of intellectual heritage, conception and duration verily exists in this manner? I have never understood why most of the people use these terms in a primitive and materialistic manner, that they are content just by having children – even though every nincompoop manages that, the fools often much more numerous and unscrupulous than other people.

Farewell, my dear – be greeted as always and ever by
Yours Marion

Chapter 5

Hopes for the 'Third Reich'

In 1930 Kurt von Plettenberg left East Prussia, 'the landscape in which he was so happy', as Marion Dönhoff will later write to his family. 'The farewell to Friedrichstein is becoming so difficult for me', he wrote in his diary on 1 September 1930. He had to part from 'East Prussia's forests and lakes, from the expansive meadows and ancient alleys'. Also the goodbye to the people pulls at his heartstrings, not only the Dönhoffs, but also to the people with whom he has worked and who were attached to him.

In Berlin where he finds an apartment in the Steglitz district, he does not settle down easily. 'Berlin is hard for me. One is nowhere as lonely as in a big city.' Also the first steps in his new job are not easy.

Since 1930, there had been a spirit of optimism in the German nationalist camp. Particularly after the elections in autumn and winter 1931/32 ministries and government agencies were deliberately infiltrated by members of the NSDAP, as was the Berlin-Brandenburg chamber of agriculture, in which Kurt von Plettenberg was promoted to head forester in May 1931. Soon National Socialists were in the majority in this agency due to the successful agitation of their farmers' leader Walter Darré.

In October 1932 Plettenberg was called into the Ministry for Food and Agriculture under Hugenberg as acting director of the forestry department of the Kurmark agricultural district, i.e. Berlin and Brandenburg. Only one-quarter of his work now involved the chamber of agriculture, so he largely avoided assimilation into the increasingly National Socialist chamber under Darré.

Like many of the later members of the resistance, among them Claus Schenk Count von Stauffenberg, Henning von Tresckow and Fritz-Dietlof Count von der Schulenburg, not to mention a large part of the German population, Plettenberg initially hoped that after the defeat of 1918 and the 'ignominious' peace with its oppressive conditions, Hitler would lead them to 'rightful greatness' again. The Nazi propaganda promising to wipe out the 'disgrace of Versailles' and to fend off the 'Bolshevist threat' have considerable impact.

Plettenberg did not become a staunch democrat during the Weimar Republic. He had no sympathy for the continual changes in government, even if some political figures of the Republic like Stegerwald, Stresemann or Otto Braun personally impressed him. Democratic forms of government did not form the principle of order to which he felt himself dedicated. On the other hand, he did not get involved in those political organisations which strove for a return to the old society by the restoration of the monarchy, let alone in the new radical-nationalist right at the forefront of which is Hitler's party and which increasingly dominates the 'national camp' towards the end of the Weimar Republic.

Plettenberg was convinced that strong personalities were better suited to lead Germany out of national and material misery than parties. That Hitler might be this personality after all, despite his previous opinions, he came to believe not least due to many conversations he had in the winter of 1932/33 with Carl-Hans Count von Hardenberg, Franz von Papen, Lutz Count Schwerin von Krosigk and others in Berlin or Neuhardenberg, which gave him 'insights into developments not available to everybody' with regard to his job at the Ministry of Food, as he noted in his diary. At the end of 1932 Plettenberg met Hindenburg in Neuhardenberg where within a small group they 'talk about the sad conflict with the NSDAP', as he wrote.

He spent the evening before Hitler's 'seizure of power' with Lutz Schwerin von Krosigk, the later Minister of Finance and husband of one of his cousins. The latter's diary notes:

> Kurt Plettenberg joined me for dinner, who told me
> Schleicher and Hammerstein were still of the opinion that the
> old man [President von Hindenburg] was no longer in full
> possession of his mental powers, and they therefore
> considered a crisis of the presidency necessary as soon as
> possible. ... Kurt shared my view that a cabinet led by Hitler
> is the only option in the current situation.

Thus Plettenberg anticipated the beginning of the new regime
with hope. The first clear remarks on Hitler's successes are to be
found in his diary two-and-a-half months after the 'seizure of
power'. On 13 April 1933 he noted: 'Hitler's victory which gives
us hope and possibilities, the indescribable rejoicing in Berlin
when the national government is at hand, the excellent opening
of the Reichstag by Hitler, the 1st assembly in the Kroll [this
means the Kroll opera house serving as a substitute for the
Reichstag which had burnt down in February] where Hitler gets
even with the pinkos.' On 26 April he wrote: 'The great political
earthquake; Hitler grows into being the great leader of the nation.
Nobody knew how great this man is after all.' And in June 1933:
'The Nazis work towards a new war. God bless the spirit of these
men who took our rescue in hand ... We must succeed in
preserving the spirit of the true Germany.'

Only very few conservatives at that time had the political and
human foresight of the experienced Kurt von Hammerstein who
from the beginning treated the National Socialists, and especially
Hitler, with disapproval. Also the Protestant milieu, in which
Plettenberg had grown up and to which he felt attached, did not
protect him from the promises of the 'Third Reich'. On the
contrary, the Protestant Church had submitted to secular rule
since the earliest days of the National Socialist government.

* * *

In the opinion of the renowned Protestant social ethicist and
contemporary historian Günter Brakelmann the majority of the
Protestant churches 'approved of the destruction of the

democratic and constitutional Weimar Republic by the "national revolution" and interpreted this "turn" as a merciful act of God in favour of the German people'. The traditional conception of statehood in favour of obedience to authority, shaped by 'anti-liberalism, anti-democracy, anti-Semitism, anti-socialism and anticommunism' fell into line without resistance with the suppression of the alleged enemies of the Christian church by the Nazi regime. They did not see through Hitler's statements about Christianity as the perfidious lies they turned out to be.

The overwhelming majority of Protestant believers and their leaders listened with enthusiasm to Hitler's speech to the German people as the new Chancellor of the Reich which was transmitted by radio on 1 February 1933. He said, among other things:

> So the national government will consider it as its chief and first task to restore the spiritual and volitional unity of our people. It will maintain and defend the foundations on which the strength of our nation is built. It will take under its protection Christianity as the basis of our entire morality and the family as the nucleus of our national and state body ...

Behind closed doors, however, the Führer struck a completely different note towards the representatives of the church. Opposition to the *Gleichschaltung* ('forced federation') of the churches, to the creation of a Reich church promoted by Hitler under the leader of the 'Faith Movement of German Christians', Reich Bishop Ludwig Müller, had meanwhile become clearly noticeable, although this resistance was only related to the reshaping of the churches.

Thirteen months after his promise to protect Christianity as basis of morality, on 13 March 1934 an angry Hitler declared bluntly to the nationalist conservative Protestant Reich bishops Wurm and Meiser on 13 March 1934:

> Christianity will vanish from Germany, as it has from Russia ... He has given the Protestant Church every chance. If the

> Church does not use it, it (the people?) will not perish. Another question is whether the institution of the church will not break because of this. The Germans existed many hundreds of thousands of years before Christ without Christianity and will live on, when Christianity has disappeared … [Meiser's notes]

Subsequently the church's resistance to *Gleichschaltung* grew, but it only aimed at safeguarding the Church's freedom from the state, its freedom of confession and preaching against totalitarian demands. The 'Confessing Church' which was beginning to take shape was no exception to this, either. There were no official church authorities which stood up for the persecuted Social Democratic, Communist or Jewish citizens and against the infringement of the personal and political freedom. Its aim was not the freedom of conscience for everybody or equality before the law. 'It [the Protestant church] never became a factor unsettling the Nazi regime at its foundations. Only individuals and small groups of Christians on their own responsibility and understanding of church resistance made the transition to political conservative resistance' was Günter Brakelmann's disillusioned assessment.

* * *

After initial enthusiasm for Hitler, Plettenberg's deliberate distancing himself from the Nationalist Socialist state grew over the years, influenced by his own experiences and observations. However, 'blunders ', which Plettenberg observes and criticises after the 'seizure of power', were not at first recognised by him as symptomatic of National Socialist politics. When his superior, chamber director Dr. Franz Mendelson, was dismissed from his office on the basis of the 'Law for the Restoration of the Professional Civil Service' of April 1933 because of his Jewish descent, Kurt von Plettenberg deeply regretted this. He wrote to him on 14 November 1933:

For me an important benchmark for the appraisal of a person of our generation is whether or rather how he acquitted himself during the war and I know from Dr. Naumann the great reputation you gained with your troops in the field …
I wish this benchmark, which thank God is in general highly honoured throughout the fatherland today, would be applied again in all cases.

Plettenberg also tried to help Mendelson find a new job in the private sector through letters of recommendation. He remained in touch with him by letter during the following years and visited him in Berlin.

Kurt von Plettenberg never became a member of the NSDAP, although he was invited to do so several times after the 'seizure of power'. 'Politically I never converted to the NSDAP. Primarily because I did not wish to shun the "Stahlhelm" in critical times', he wrote to Count Arnim-Muskau in October 1933. During the Weimar Republic he had belonged, like many of his social class and friends, to the Stahlhelm', a league of former front soldiers founded by Franz Seldte, who was involved in the organisation's gradual subordination to the SA, culminating in its circa one million members becoming SA Reserve I in November 1933. Because of this, Plettenberg sought to resign from the Stalhelm, as he told his friend Hardenberg.

To Baron Rüdt von Collenberg of the Board of the German Associations of Forest Owners, who urged him in May 1933 to join the Party, he wrote that he could not join the NSDAP at that moment, 'as much as I wish Hitler and his associates the best outcome of all their endeavours, as much as I am convinced of the general rightness of their programmes. Even the errors which I believe to detect in individual economic and political measures would not hinder, but rather encourage, me to join the NSDAP. Yet I cannot come over at a time, when such savage attacks by the press are directed against Rohr, who is after all my superior, and who I furthermore consider to be a perfectly decent man'. The loyalty which Plettenberg showed the Secretary of State in the Ministry for Food Hansjoachim von Rohr (German People's Party), a Pomeranian lord of the manor and friend of his future father-in-law Helmuth von Maltzahn, was also directed against the attempts of the agricultural and forestry apparatus of the NSDAP to deprive von Rohr of his power. Hitler himself had called for von Rohr to receive the leading agricultural politicians of the NSDAP and to formulate his policy with them. Von Rohr had declined to do so with the plain statement that he did not conduct such negotiations with party representatives on principle. As a consequence, Hitler pursued his dismissal. It followed after Hugenberg's resignation under the latter's successor Darré, after von Rohr had criticised his minister's positions on agricultural policy and the NSDAP in a public speech.

Despite this solidarity with the political position of his superior, Plettenberg sympathised with parts of the NSDAP programme, especially with Item 17 which planned the expropriation of large landowners. In the above-mentioned letter dated October 1933 to Count Arnim-Muskau he wrote:

> Yet I see clearly that in this day and age the tendency of the state government in power is in general not friendly towards the very large land owners, and I admit that regarding this issue I have always been of the opinion with Heini Dönhoff that I personally, if I see matters from the point of view of state government, do not consider the preservation of very large land ownership as one of the most important tasks of the state, if means and ways were found to create healthier social conditions by the partition of such estates. ...

In Plettenberg's opinion an exception should be made for large forest ownership, though. Hereby he certainly thought of the necessity of expert hunting and gamekeeping which cannot be managed on a small scale.

In the deliberations on the future of large land ownership Plettenberg's hopes for a more humane economic life meet the 'socialist' tendencies of the NSDAP programme. His social attitudes become even clearer later in the letter:

> In particular I am entirely convinced that not just mercantile calculation and political skill should decide the fate of our fatherland, but that human relationships and the conscious responsibility of the economic leaders for the people entrusted to them will play a decisive role. I believe that a certain warmth can be brought to the work also in a large enterprise by personal initiative and influence on the employees of all kinds, by the commitment to human solidarity and community of fate of all people working there, which will have a beneficial effect in every way on the enterprise and perhaps even on a larger scale beyond. I believe ... that my view on the position of the employee and in particular of the worker in the company fits into the framework of the current development, and if I wonder at, and am often even vexed about some of what is happening in Germany today, I see in this respect much good and much promising work.

As much as he initially believed in the social pronouncements of the Nazi programme, his resistance to the political-power demand of the regime increased, particularly in those years of *Gleichschaltung*. He attempted to prevent the *Akademischen Feldjägergesellschaften* (AFG – Academic Hunting Society) becoming part of the National Socialist German Students' League. While he was studying forestry Plettenberg had become a member of this organisation which emerged from the *Reitenden Feldjägerkorps* (Mounted Huntsmen's Corps), after university continuing his membership as an 'old boy'.

At the decisive members' meeting of the society in November 1935, where either the dissolution or the merger of the AFG into the National Socialist German Students' League was up for debate, according to the minutes only a few members speak against the merger and for the dissolution of the AFG, among them Kurt von Plettenberg. The leader of the majority in the assembly hall, the National Socialist Malte von Engelbrecht, later described his impression: 'Kurt Baron von Plettenberg was by far the best speaker against me. Abundantly clear, in a courtly manner, logical and convincing. With him a world view stood against me.'

Engelbrecht, a member of the National Socialist German Students' League, sensed the principle behind the rejection of the conservative faction. A slim majority finally voted for Engelbrecht's motion. The AFG then continued to exist only as an old boy's club, but met regularly for conventions. Until his death in 1938 Plettenberg's father Karl participated in these as the former commander of the Mounted 'Feldjäger' Corps (1902–6) and simultaneously its honorary chairman.

Later, during his time as president of the court chamber of the house of Schaumburg-Lippe, Plettenberg refused all invitations to Party events, pleading pressure of work. Hereby he was certainly led by his growing distance from the regime, but which he does not wish to state publicly, however, in the interests of his employer. It would increase even further later during his career in the Reich forestry office under Göring, until he finally quited public service for good.

During these early years in Berlin, especially after the experiences which he had during the seizure of power by Hitler, Kurt von Plettenberg's political opinion evidently changed. He recognised more and more the kind of situation the Germans had got themselves into, when they trusted the Führer. These experiences were the preconditions for his finding his way into the resistance.

Chapter 6

Arianne
Baroness von Maltzahn

The 1930s were a time of change for Kurt von Plettenberg not only politically and professionally, but also fundamentally in his private life. At first the friendless head forester found it difficult to settle in in Berlin. He not only lamented the lack of human companionship, but also experienced the city as a place where 'God can no longer be as close to a person as through nature'.

It was his friendship with an old war comrade, Carl-Hans von Hardenberg, which gave him back the longed-for access to nature and loving people, a kind of second Friedrichstein. As often as possible he fled the city and his desk and let his chauffeur Bernhard drive him in his red cabriolet to the Hardenbergs at Neuhardenberg in the Mark of Brandenburg. 'In Neuhardenberg often happy hours, because the people there surround me with love and the children relax and delight me', he wrote in his diary at the end of 1932.

Reinhild, Hardenberg's third daughter, known as Wonte, recalled these encounters from the children's perspective in her autobiography:

> Among the great joys of my childhood and youth counted the visits by Kurt Plettenberg – Uncle Kürtchen. He was our favourite guest and was dearly beloved by all family members equally and unconditionally. Already as very little

71

girls we sisters made the decision independently from each other to later marry nobody else but Uncle Kürtchen. He himself was particularly fond of my youngest sister Atti. The great affection which we had for him founded in the manner he made an effort with us. He never brought us sweets – he was the only one among our guests of whom we did not expect this – instead he responded to all our concerns. He gave comfort and advice: he simply took us seriously.

Reinhild Hardenberg shared this experience with Marion Dönhoff who had found it equally astonishing how he – almost twenty years older – was talking seriously to her, a young girl. In another passage, Wonte describes him as follows:

Kurt Plettenberg had been a close and trusted friend of my father since the First World War. He had medium blond hair and wore glasses with thick lenses. When he took off the glasses occasionally, his eyes changed dramatically which usually looked at us so firmly. He suddenly seemed self-conscious and shy, even vulnerable, which neither fitted his normal appearance nor his manner.

Was his astonishing popularity perhaps the result of a struggle to hide a deeper layer of unease and sorrow? It was the code of conduct of the landed nobility to be good company and not to embarrass one's social circle with personal problems. In Neuhardenberg a special humour prevailed. 'You are the saucisson among the sausages, my dear Hanni, among the princes!', Plettenberg telegraphed on the occasion of his friend being made a 'prince'.

The search for a suitable woman became more and more pressing for Plettenberg, by then already 39 years old. From a cure at Carlsbad little had remained in his mind. 'Many girls who are peculiarly eager in their interest in me. However, what actually sticks in my mind is only – <u>wonderful</u> nature! His diary reads: In a letter to his confidant, his cousin Elisabeth, he lamented his loneliness resulting from the lack of a permanent bond: 'If I was married, I would in the end not feel so much, which I now perceive with an almost feverishly increasing intensity, the fact of being entirely without roots.' And in his diary he wrote: 'They are all attentive to me, perhaps they sense how desperate I often am behind my mask which I have kept already since twenty years or more since early childhood.'

The splendid summer of 1929 which he had enjoyed – still in East Prussia – especially during rides on the Courland Spit, had a particular afterglow, 'because Sissi was so charming', but he learnt that he had come too late. A little later Sissi Lehndorff from Preyl was engaged and married Dieter, the second oldest Dönhoff in Friedrichstein. He confided in his diary: 'What will become of me, if I remain a bachelor without hope for the future, I do not know.'

His social upbringing set limits to his choice of a wife:

> And I during the last months? My little 'Bavarian love' becomes suddenly very important and I begin to seriously consider whether it is not right to throw overboard all the slightly dubious, though in principle justified stuff of tradition and social order for the love of my true person. I have experienced some happy hours, the happiest of my life so far.

He found distraction in a two-week road trip with some friends. It led him in spring 1933 through the whole of Italy via Rome down to Sicily. He saw Taormina, Etna and Palermo, and took the ship back to Naples where he visited Pompeii, Sorrento and the Amalfi coast. Through Etruria they travel back to Munich via Milan, Como and Lucerne. Plettenberg was enchanted and rhapsodised about the splendid landscape of Calabria and Sicily, about the churches and palaces.

Yet very soon the exhilarating inspiration faded into the hectic Berlin working life: 'Like a dream the journey lies behind me.' Then, finally, at the beginning of 1934 in Neuhardenberg he met

Arianne von Maltzahn, a schoolfriend of Hardenberg's oldest daughter, who had been invited to Neuhardenberg castle for the weekend. Everybody gathered for dinner around a long, white-covered table, and Arianne leans slightly forward to say something to the person sitting opposite her. Kurt von Plettenberg, seated at the head of the table, noticed her well-formed profile and he said to his friend Hanni Hardenberg: 'I will marry her!' To which the latter replies: 'Her name is Arianne von Maltzahn. You better let it be, as you will only get a parcel of sausages for Christmas, her parents have eight children!'

Arianne, born in Potsdam, grew up on a little estate, Schossow in the Demmin district in Western Pomerania. She was not the typical rural child who played around outside 'near the stables' like her younger siblings. She preferred to withdraw from the boisterous little ones and bury herself in her books.

She was the second oldest of eight children of Helmuth von Maltzahn and his wife Freda von Arnim. Arianne's grandfather had been Secretary of State for the Treasury (Minister of Finance) under Bismarck and Caprivi, and then became governor of Pomerania. Arianne's father did not wish to work for the Republic and, therefore, managed the Schossow estate after his retirement from public service in 1919. He was active in the Pomeranian Rural Federation. As a deeply religious Protestant and active member of the Confessing Church, he could not reconcile himself to the Nazis. He is close to the chairman of the Rural Federation, Hansjoachim von Rohr, who had anti-Nazi views and who in 1931 was Secretary of State in the Reich Ministry of Food under Hugenberg and thus Kurt von Plettenberg's superior. Because of his uncompromising attitude towards the politically-motivated demands of the NSDAP, he was removed from office on Hitler's instigation soon after 1933, as mentioned above.

Arianne's mother came from the house of Arnim-Neuensund. Early in life she lost her mother who had suffered from poor health for a long time. Therefore, she, as the oldest daughter, had to take over the management of the large household of the estate at a young age. Perhaps this early burden was the cause for her strictness with her eight children and the staff in Schossow. Yet Freda von Maltzahn had many interests, and took part in the politics of the day. She must have been one of the few women who had actually read Hitler's *Mein Kampf*.

During the presidential election campaign she complained that the candidate of the German Nationalists, Theodor Duesterberg, had such a slight chance against Hindenburg. From a letter dated 25 January 1932 to her daughter Arianne about the results of the state elections in the three constituencies where her husband and his two brothers had their estates, it becomes clear that the German Nationals received almost more than three times as many votes as the National Socialists.

She also mentioned the so-called 'Potsdam Day', 21 March 1933, in a letter. On this day Hitler and Hindenburg met in front of the Garrison Church in Potsdam on the occasion of the opening of the Reichstag. They demonstrated the reconciliation of the national-conservative camp with the NSDAP and Hitler publicly received Hindenburg's 'blessing'. Freda von Maltzahn wrote to Arianne: 'Unfortunately the Nazis have sidelined Bruno Walter, which I deeply regret because of his abilities. In general "cronyism" seems to have started.' On 15 March 1933 we read in a letter by her: 'Now such grave issues are raised everywhere due to *Gleichschaltung*. In terms of foreign politics the situation seems hopeless, and as Papen says, just like 1914 we are encircled. I have such dread of war, as it will now unfold.' On 28 June 1933 she added: 'Today it was said that Hugenberg had resigned, then Hansjoachim von Rohr will of course fall, too, and Darré has achieved his goal, so woe betide the large estates.'

When Kurt von Plettenberg saw Arianne in Neuhardenberg and fell in love with her, she was about to graduate from the municipal Oberlyzeum, the girls' grammar school of Eberswalde. In term-time she lived, like almost all children from the countryside, in a boarding school in town. She passed her *Abitur* as the best of her year 'accidentally with "distinction"', as she wrote in a letter to her former governess. Arianne's particular love was for music. She played the piano very well, sang and in addition was learning to play the viola, because this instrument was missing from her boarding school's small orchestra.

Arianne's headmistresses knew before Arianne herself that Plettenberg had taken a serious interest in her, from the fact that they saw him running 'at a fast gallop' to the café where they were meeting. From then on Arianne's favourite cake was 'Eberswald cruller'. Plettenberg had regular business in Eberswald and regularly attended the meetings of the administrative council of the Society for Forestry Utilisation and Work Science there. After gossip spread around the boarding school, however, both preferred meeting in Neuhardenberg.

In March 1934 Plettenberg wrote still a little hesitantly in his diary: 'Furthermore I have the intention – yet again – to marry. Yet this time it is serious. Hopefully it will succeed. I believe that despite the great difference in age many sureties are given.' On 27 July he confided in his diary:

> My entire world view has changed. I feel free and happy inside, for – I am very, very happily engaged. My dearly beloved Nannilein has been given to me by God and I know that I can only be grateful. I actually got engaged on the 22nd, officially on the 28th of April, and since then have enjoyed boundless happiness and internal joy – heartfelt joy. As grave as the concerns for the fatherland are, I am full of personal peace as never before in my life and know I will be better able to work and fight than before.

Despite her youth, Arianne also seems to have felt that she had found the right one, and this feeling will not leave her even in the following years, as her letters to her 'Kurdel' show. She wrote to her former governess:

> Yes, and now I am engaged. I am sorry that I cannot present my Kurt to you, as you would certainly like him very much. He is a particularly splendid person. Unfortunately, though I

myself do not perceive or feel this anymore, he is 23 years older than me, hence already 43. Yet he still looks very young and especially his manner is such that one forgets his age entirely. Last weekend he was here in Schossow for the first time. These were wonderful days, everything was so beautiful. He fits perfectly to Schossow and gets along swimmingly with Father, about which I am particularly happy.

Arianne's parents, likewise, did not mind the age difference between the couple, as her father was himself 19 years older than her mother. This was not unusual at that time. During the summer months the tone of Plettenberg's letters to Arianne became more intimate. The distant 'Dear Mademoiselle' turns into 'My dearly beloved Nannilein' after the engagement. They wrote to each other very frequently, as Kurt was very often away on business. On 4 September 1934 the wedding took place in Schossow. Kurt invited his best friends to the celebration: Heinrich Dönhoff from Friedrichstein, the brothers Carl-Hans and Wilfried Hardenberg and a university friend, the forester Karl-Peter Rheinen. The wedding photo shows how young the female friends of the bride are in comparison to the groom's friends. The clergyman, a relative of the bride, recited a poem by Christian Morgenstern for the couple and their future common path in life, because Kurt was particularly fond of the poet and also because the poem reflected the bond of the young couple particularly well. Both were rooted in a Christian tradition which did not feel bound by dogmatic rules, but wished to follow one's own conscience.

The others are so many,
You only enter into a game,
Which will never come to rest again.
Just walk God's path,
Let nothing else be your guide,
So that you may walk straight and narrow,
Even if you are walking on your own.

The toasts at the wedding vividly demonstrated the spirit and values Kurt and the young Arianne had been brought up with. Although the republic had replaced the monarchy and the emperor was living in exile in Holland far removed from any political power, on the evening of the wedding the father of the bride Helmuth von Maltzahn's first toast of the evening is: 'To the Prussian royal house and hurrah to His Majesty the emperor and king!'

Kurt's father, old General von Plettenberg, adorns his speech with martial and chivalrous images and links God's blessing not only with the culture of the couple's attentiveness in their life together, but with the nobility of their descent:

> You, my dear son, are today giving your hand in marriage to a daughter from a noble Pomeranian family who like us on Westphalia's red soil has resided a good millennium on their land and maintained their sacred traditions, whose golden spurs men have borne through the millennia, their hands on their swords, the foot in the stirrup, faithful to their celestial and earthly lord.

Regarding the disenfranchisement of the nobility after the war, he continues: 'And if the leadership role is more and more taken from us, so we will regain it by faithful toil. 'In this wedding speech, in which he talks about the duties the aristocracy must fulfil, the old general displayed a consciousness of tradition from which the strength to resist might spring if the circumstances made it necessary. Carl-Hans Count Hardenberg toasted his friend at the end of his speech: 'We believe in you as the embodiment of the best of the Prussian spirit.'

Naturally the question arises how much the daily family life of the young couple was actually influenced by the 'belief of the fathers'. Yet certainly these values were something held in respect. However, it also may be that they already created a little distance between them.

Arianne's mother dominated the first months of marriage – evident from some preserved correspondence – and young

Arianne had some difficulty in establishing her independence. But the couple soon moved to their own apartment in Berlin-Charlottenburg and lead a harmonious marriage. Arianne, as a former 'peasant baroness' and having just left school, initially felt slightly insecure faced with the older, established friends of her husband, as she wanted to do everything right: 'How you do it in your household, Arianne, so it is always right', said her guest Carl-Hans Hardenberg to her fondly.

In their three and half years of married life in Berlin, Arianne met a number of Plettenberg's close friends and acquaintances who were united in opposition to the Nazis and later in resistance to the regime. During dinner anything is discussed, especially current politics. Kurt finds in his young wife a serious, musically-gifted woman interested in literature and politics, who is sensitive and empathic and who cares for him lovingly. For him it was important that intellectual dialogue is possible despite her youth. Finally he has his bond, his social nest, his own family: on 19 December 1936 their daughter Christa-Erika is born in Berlin.

Nevertheless urban life is anything but easy for Arianne von Plettenberg. Asta, a friend from boarding school, the sister of Helmuth James Count von Moltke, later told her children that as a young mother Arianne was often alone in Berlin, because of her husband's obligations due to his executive post in the Reich Forestry Office. Daily life certainly demanded great adjustment from the young woman who moved shortly after her *Abitur* from a provincial boarding school to the capital without professional training. Letters written by the couple at short intervals had to replace the togetherness all too often impossible.

Chapter 7

Resignation from Public Service

After the Nazis' 'seizure of power' on 30 January 1933 an open power struggle broke out for the control of forestry policy. The protagonists were Walter Darré and Hermann Göring. Darré had become the new Minister for Food and Agriculture on 29 June 1933, succeeding Hugenberg, and in addition now claimed the entire forestry sector for himself which he wanted to turn into a subordinate department of his agricultural administration. Already by May 1933 Darré, the 'Reich Leader of Farmers', had integrated not only all agricultural, but also all forestry associations, the chambers of agriculture and agricultural cooperatives into his 'Office for Agrarian Policy of the NSDAP' and created the *Reichsnährstand* (statutory corporation of farmers in Nazi Germany) by legislation in September, which was supposed to adopt measures for regulating markets and the prices of all agricultural products. Disguise as self-management, the compulsory membership in the *Reichsnährstand* encompassed all personnel and organisations in this sector.

This brought Darré into conflict with Göring. At first acting Prussian Minister of the Interior and from 20 April 1933 also Minister-President of Prussia, Göring had taken control of the Prussian state forestry administration and assumed the title of Prussian state forester. He was also looking to expand his authority. His interest in forestry primarily derived from his passion for hunting. He succeeded in convincing Hitler and his cabinet that responsibility for forestry and gamekeeping had to be transferred to the Reich. Göring had originally planned on becoming minister, but was not successful in this, only becoming the head of the 'Reich Forestry Office', although he, therefore, was the de facto equivalent Reich minister. From 3 July 1934 onwards he could revel in the newly-created title of 'Reich Forester and Reich Huntsman' and began to deprive Darré's forestry department in the *Reichsnährstand* of its power in favour of the Reich Forestry Office.

After Göring had merged the Prussian state forest administration with the new Reich Forestry Office, he was based in a new building in the centre of Berlin at the Leipziger Platz. Walter von Keudell took over the directorship of the entire forest and timber management in the Reich Forestry Office. Keudell, in the 1920s chairman of the association of Prussian forest owners, had temporarily been Reich Minister of the Interior and joined the NSDAP after the 'seizure of power' for career reasons. In 1934 he was appointed General Head Forester with the rank of a State Secretary. With this, the highest position in the administration after Göring had been given to a man who had not completed the typical civil service career. This did not make him popular, as later controversies affecting him demonstrated. To this was added, as the forestry historian Heinrich Rubner wrote, that this musically-interested man was considered by many as too soft despite his passion for hunting. His reputation was primarily based on the fact that he advocated as an economic principle the ecologically-oriented form of forest management which he had successfully practised for many years on his estate at Hohenlübbichow. Keudell promoted the avoidance of clear-felling which was particularly common in coniferous forests. Instead he argued for 'selective cutting' which should only take place every two to three years. With this Keudell strove for a reorientation in favour of forestry closer to nature, which could allow better recover felling. In the medium term even higher output could be achieved with this method.

In 1936 Hermann Göring was appointed 'Commissioner of the Führer' for the Four-Year Plan. This extended Göring's powers of economic planning and management, also for that of forest and timber management in the Reich. His efforts were now primarily directed towards increased autonomy of the German economy as regarded resources. Subsequently forestry became an instrument of armament planning. The increased demand for wood as an important raw material for the accelerating rearmament threatened Keudell's previous sustainable forestry policies. The latter had forbidden the felling of immature coniferous populations younger than 50 years on the basis of the 'Reich Law against Forest Devastation' of 1934.

Göring's speech to the German Forestry Association setting out his programme in August 1936, in which he called the forest an organism 'whose treatment and management has to be adapted to its biological requirements', had still been based on Keudell's ideas. Natural rejuvenation and orientation towards mixed forests were named as goals, as were stock maintenance and care for future growth. This was summed up in the slogan the 'Preservation of the German forest in its importance for the people and national culture'. In the forest exhibition of 1936 in Berlin and in the film *Perpetual Forest, Perpetual People* of the same year 'trees of foreign species' in German forests were condemned and the 'German forest people' was distinguished from the 'Slavic steppe people' and the 'Jewish desert people'! A few years later signs were put up at the edge of the forests: 'Jews are not welcome in our German forests.'

In contrast to this propaganda backdrop, the reality was summed up in Göring's statement: 'We have to get as much out of the German forest as possible.' It became clearer and clearer that with this Keudell's never-uncontroversial forest policies came into conflict with the aims of economic autarky of the Reich leadership. Against his wishes, Göring had demanded a 50 per cent increase of the annual cut in the state forests soon after his appointment as Reichsjägermeister (Reich Master of the Hunt), which could not be reconciled with Keudell's policy of single-tree selection. Keudell's uncompromising attitude towards the critics of the permanent forest concept rapidly weakened his position. Göring secretly pursued his removal which followed at the end of 1937. Keudell's forestry decrees were rescinded shortly afterwards.

* * *

From October 1932 Kurt von Plettenberg was acting head of the forestry department of the agricultural province of Kurmark and also worked in the Reich Ministry of Food and Agriculture headed by Hugenberg. In 1934 he was called to Göring's Reich State Forestry Office. On the occasion of his retirement from the Ministry he wanted to make suggestions concerning his successor to the state secretary in charge Willy Parchmann, a National Socialist. Parchmann rejected this brusquely: 'Such positions are only available to gentlemen I personally have evaluated thoroughly, who I know very well', i.e. Nazi Party members.

In the Reich State Forestry Office Kurt von Plettenberg initially worked as an aide and from October 1934 with his appointment as county forester and head of the important budget department for Keudell. In the Reich Forestry Office Plettenberg stumbled into the controversies regarding the future of forest management. He sympathised with Keudell's concept of natural increase in value of the forest, which had also been advocated by some of his teachers at the forestry academies in Hannoversch-Münden and Eberswalde. He reported to his cousin Elisabeth von Sydow at the end of 1934 that he had to assert himself against 'economic and political resistance' in the office.

According to Erich Koennecke, Keudell's personal assistant, Plettenberg was discussed as a potential replacement for Keudell when he was deposed by Göring, a claim which is supported by Andreas Gautschi in his study *The Reich Huntsman. Facts and Legends around Hermann Göring*. Plettenberg himself later confirmed that some 'well-meaning persons have made the attempt and that it was apparently discussed for a while'. Yet he had already decided otherwise. The exploitation of forestry for rearmament, which would force him to collaborate in the devastation of the German forests in the interests of the war economy, was impossible for him. In the presence of his sister he spoke out with the drastic words: 'I won't let myself be turned into the butcher of the German forests.' These experiences he had in his professional life under the Nazis increased his distance from the new regime. His decision to resign from public service was a foregone conclusion.

Plettenberg resigned from the Reich Forestry Office in October 1937. Luckily, an opportunity had arisen that made it easy for him to quit public service. Since the beginning of the year, Wolrad zu Schaumburg-Lippe, head of the former princely house and a comrade from the 2nd Guard Uhlans, had been trying to engage Plettenberg as the manager of his estate, which was in financial difficulties. Plettenberg decided to take the job as president of the court chamber in Bückeburg, but as he had a family to provide for, he took the precaution of not leaving the security of the civil service straight away, initially arranging a period of administrative leave. As he wrote to Keudell in his application for administrative leave, the estate comprised 'a great forest property of which circa 5,000 ha are in Schaumburg-Lippe, 2,500 ha in Mecklenburg and 10,000 ha in Austria. The administration furthermore encompasses circa 26,000 acres of agricultural enterprises and extensive property in castles and houses.'

At the beginning of July 1937 Göring orders Plettenberg to Karinhall to discuss his reasons for resigning from public service on 1 October and his future prospects. Plettenberg reports the decisive conversation with Göring to his direct superior Keudell 'according to instructions': 'In response I presented him with a letter from the Prince zu Schaumburg-Lippe addressed to him, in which the prince requested my resignation from public service with the assurance of a right to return.' After Göring had appraised himself of the details, he said 'that he wholly understands the occupation as senior official in this administration would be more satisfying to me than a desk job in Berlin and that he does not wish to put obstacles in my way. Furthermore he would be willing to assure me of a right to return to public service …' With his appointment as Senior State Forester (Oberlandforstmeister) in autumn 1937

Plettenberg left the Reich Forestry Office and took on the administration of the court chamber in Bückeburg.

In his inaugural speech to the staff he recalled his family ties to Bückeburg and its princely house for which his father had served as commander of the Bückeburg Jäger and where he himself was born. He then emphasised 'that any ownership of land is a fiefdom for the general population and that from this special duties arise for the respective owner; duties to manage his property in a manner best for the fatherland.'

Plettenberg took over the management in difficult circumstances, as Schwertfeger, the legal advisor of the princely house and his closest colleague, reported after the war: 'Heavy burdens rested on the assets, the interest largely ate up the annual income. Therefore, a radical reorganisation was necessary right away.' In particular, the large Austrian estate in Steyrling had become entirely out of hand due to unfavourable contracts with the tenants and had to be brought back under the control of the court chamber through difficult negotiations. In Bückeburg 'unpleasant staffing arrangements' had to be sorted out. The landed estate in Mecklenburg, the management of property in Berlin, Munich and Bonn, to which the 'Palais Schaumburg' also belonged, required exhausting travel. To this was added the legal dispute over the compensation which the head of the house of Schaumburg-Lippe had to pay to his brothers after the end of the entailed estate.

With Plettenberg's move to Bückeburg his family's time in Berlin came to an end and they moved into a spacious rented house in the southern part of the town. Their son Karl-Wilhelm was born there in March 1938. In the same year Kurt's parents died shortly after one another in Bückeburg. A little street which leads off Georgstraße immediately next to the home of the young family was named 'Plettenbergstraße' by the town council of Bückeburg, in honour of the highly-esteemed old general. Some years later, in 1943, their youngest daughter Dorothea-Marion was also born in Bückeburg.

His new job allowed him less time for his family than he would have wished, but the reorganisation of the properties of the house of Schaumburg-Lippe made great progress in the following years. Plettenberg also continued to be active in the Society for Forest Utilisation and Work Science in Eberswalde and on the main committee for Forest Seed Certification, although this was dissolved in 1939. On the committee for Forestry Policy of the German Forestry association he represents the interests of the large private forest owners against the attempts of the state authorities to infringe upon their rights. The latter saw Plettenberg, a former senior civil servant in the Reich Forestry Office, as a competent advisor who had the necessary knowledge and contacts to represent their interests.

The danger of estates being broken up after the abolition of entails had to be prevented, as high inheritance taxes collectively threatened the estates. Plettenberg, therefore, appealed to the Reich Minister of Finance Schwerin von Krosigk for exemptions from inheritance tax for forest owners, arguing that otherwise forest property would become inefficient or at risk of financial speculation. In the case of smaller forest properties, he supported the plans to form them into cooperatives.

For him the question of lumber prices being fixed too low in comparison to the tax burden on the business was inseparable from the preservation of large, cohesively managed forest areas. With the outbreak of the war this problem was increasingly exacerbated by the overcutting demanded by the state. The coercion to turn wood into money in this manner combined with special taxes was in his opinion not only an inadmissible infringement on private property, but also a disaster for the forests which no longer can sufficiently endure damage by storms and insects due to worsening brushwood regeneration, 'as furthermore a decline and devaluation of the soil occurs due to an overuse of paths and due to tardy and deficiently executed cultivation, as in short in almost all woodlands known to me the overall state of the forests, which have been built up with careful

Above left: A depiction of Wolter von Plettenberg (1660-1553) Landmaster of the Teutonic Knights; Imperial Prince, on a stone relief, ca. 1515 in the courtyard of Marienburg castle, Riga. Above right: An enlarged portrait, cast from the relief-statue, of Wolter von Plettenberg.

Above left: The father: Kurt Freiherr von Plettenberg Com. General of the Guard Corps (1916) Above right: The mother: Clara Freifrau von Plettenberg, née Countess von Wedel.

Above: The brothers: Karl-Wilhelm and Kurt von Plettenberg, aged 12 and 10 respectively, pictured in 1914

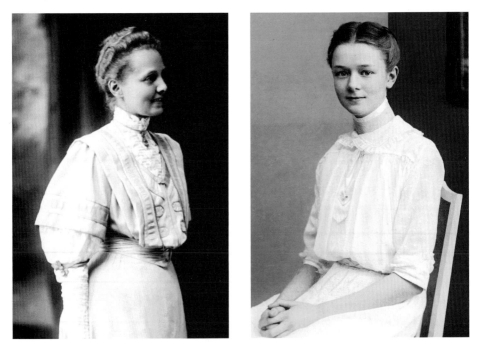

Above left: The mother Clara Freifrau von Plettenberg aged 31. Above right: The sister Luise Baroness von Plettenberg.

Above left: Favourite cousin Elisabeth von Sydow, longstanding confident of Kurt von Plettenberg. Above right: A young Kurt von Plettenberg after a successful hunt.

Above: Generalmajor Karl von Plettenberg (right) takes a parade in Colmar, Elsass, of 14. Hunters Batallion infront of Duke Johann Albrecht von Mecklenburg (left) before World War I.

Above: 1905, Rgt. Commanders congratulate Duke Leopold zu Hohenzollern-Sigmaringen, Com. General of the 1st foot Guards Rgt. (second from left) on his 70th birthday; Karl Freiherr von Plettenberg is to be seen third from left, standing in front, brothers Karl-Wilhelm and Kurt von Plettenberg

Above left: Emperor Wilhelm II and his adjutant general Karl Frhr.v.Plettenberg during a military exercise c.1913/1914. Above right: With the 6th Army: Com. General Sixt von Arnim (2nd.from right) with Karl Frhr. von Plettenberg (3rd from right) along with Fieldmarshall Crownprince Rupprecht von Bayern (centre).

Above: Siegfried Graf von Eulenburg-Wicken, last Commander of the 1st foot Guards Rgt; lifelong friend of Kurt von Plettenberg. Top right: Kurt von Plettenberg lieutenant in 2rd Guards-Ulanen Rgt. and (right) Karl-Wilhelm von Plettenberg as a lieutenant in 1st foot Guards Rgt.

Above left: Emperor Wilhelm II between General a la suite Friedrich von Friedeburg and his general adjutant, Karl Freiherr von Plettenberg, in Potsdam 1913. Above right: Karl Frhr.von Plettenberg in Paradeuniform and wearing the ribbon of the Red Eagle Order with oak-leafes after World War I in Bückeburg.

Above: General Karl von Plettenberg having laid a wreath at the Semper Talis, Memorial to the 1st foot Guard Rgt. (and flank companies) next to the Garrison-Church, Potsdam 1926.

Above: Von Plettenberg during a bear-hunting expedition in the Carpathian mountains, Rumania, summer 1929.

Above left: Marion Countess Dönhoff in Eastprussia c.1928. Above right: Von Plettenberg with his hunting dog Wotan c.1925. Below: Kurt von Plettenberg in Berlin 1931 with friends.

Above: A meeting at the Prussian Forestry administration, Berlin 1931. Last row 4th from left Carl-Hans Graf von Hardenberg, Franz von Mendelsson (5th from left), head of chamber for agriculture. Kurt von Plettenberg (head of forestry department) can be seen 2nd from right.

Above left: The engaged couple Arianne von Maltzahn and Kurt von Plettenberg and (above right) the newly wedded couple at Schossow, Pomerania.

Above left: Arianne Freifrau von Plettenberg c.1937. Above right: Von Plettenberg father-in-law, Helmuth Freiherr von Maltzahn, in Schossow, autumn 1938

Above: Schossow Manor-House, of the von Maltzahn family, in former rural district Demmin, Pomerania.

Above: The bride and groom Arianne and Kurt von Plettenberg with their wedding guests at Schossow, 4 September 1934. Below: Clara and Karl von Plettenberg with the circle of their closest relatives, among them Kurt and Arianne with their daughter Christa (back row left), Bückeburg 1936.

Above left: Sandfort castle of the Graf von Wedel family in Westphalia, birthplace of Clara von Plettenberg, née Countess von Wedel. Above right: Major Kurt von Plettenberg 1939. Below left: Kurt von Plettenberg during a military sports event held by his regiment in 1940. Below right: Von Plettenberg before crossing a river during operation *Barbarossa*, 1941.

Above left and right: Von Plettenbergphotographed whilst commander of 415 Regiment on the Eastern Front, Russia, during the winter of 1941. Below: Neuhardenberg castle, a meeting place for conspirators planning the *Valkyrie* plot.

Above: The friends Carl-Hans Count von Hardenberg, owner of Neuhardenberg, pictured with (left), Karl-Peter Rheinen (forester) and Kurt Freiherr von Plettenberg (right) on the Western front, Elsass, 1940. Above right: Axel Freiherr von dem Bussche.

Above left: Claus Schenk Graf von Stauffenberg (shot 20 July 1944). Above right: Hening von Tresckow (committed suicide 2. July 1944).

Above left: Carl Hans Graf von Hardenberg (he survived imprisonment). Above right: Reinhild Countess von Hardenberg, fiancé of Stauffenbergs adjudant Werner von Haeften, (she survived imprisonment). Below left: Fritz-Dietloff Graf von der Schulenburg (executed 10 August 1944 in Berlin-Plötzensee). Below right:Fabian von Schlabrendorff (he survived torture and imprisonment).

Left: Prince Louis Ferdinand von Preussen (1907 – 1994) former family-head of the Hohenzollerns and (above) The Prussian royal crown, from 1889, which Kurt von Plettenberg hid 1945 in the village church of Kleinenbremen, near Bückeburg, to secure the crown from confiscation by the Russian Army.

Below left: The Dutch Palace, Unter den Linden, Berlin. Kurt von Plettenberg originally had his office in this palace, which was badly bombed during a bombing raid in November 1943. It was partially rebuilt in the former DDR after World War II. Below right: Gestapo prison at No. 8 Prince Albrecht -Street in Berlin; badly damaged by bombs and torn down after the War.

Above left: Kurt von Plettenberg with his children Christa- Erika, Dorothea- Marion (in his arms) and Karl-Wilhelm, 1944. Above right: Christa-Erika, Dorothea-Marion and Karl-Wilhelm von Plettenberg in Bückeburg 1947. Below: Tombstone in Bornstedt cemetery, close to Sancoussi, Potsdam.

treatment by generations exercising a modest way of life, has increasingly deteriorated ...'.

This continuing concern for the forests, not just economically motivated, caused Plettenberg in 1938 to campaign for an independent Reich Forestry Chamber on a federal basis made up of the Reich Forestry Office and some of the large forest owners. With this, the owners would be to collaborate securely with the civil service. Such a representation of their interests seemed all the more important to him, after Göring spoke against the continuing resistance of the *Reichsnährstand*: 'I must determine how the German forests – regardless where – are managed to secure the highest proceeds.' As a member in the committee for forestry policy Plettenberg defended his position vigorously in memoranda and meetings with Keudell's successor, General Head Forester Friedrich Alpers. He also tried to influence the Reich forestry law, which was still in the drafting stage, in that direction. Yet in the end he was unsuccessful, because no decision was made on it due to the war and the drafts were filed away.

How much his advice was sought after was also shown when he was asked to mediate in the sale of the imperially-owned Rominter Heath to the Prussian state. In December 1938 the general agent of the former Prussian royal house, the retired General von Dommes, approached him and asked him to take on the role of arbitrator in all disputes which might arise from contracts regarding the estate of the Prussian royal house. In these contracts, Emperor Wilhelm, in exile in Holland, had provisionally relinquished his personal assets in Germany in form of real estate, castles etc. to his son, Crown Prince Wilhelm. The Crown Prince himself submitted to similar legal conditions in favour of the other members of the family. In an arbitration agreement it is settled:

> All disputes and questions regarding the interpretation and execution of the principal contract mentioned above, which arise between the signatory parties, shall be settled under

> exclusion of ordinary legal proceedings by an arbitrating body, for which a special arrangement shall be made ... The arbitrating body shall consist of the president of the court chamber Baron von Plettenberg in Bückeburg as permanent arbitrator.

This was undoubtedly a great mark of confidence in Plettenberg, who would thus act as arbitrator in disputes between the numerous members of the former Prussian royal house, which were likely to arise given the still-considerable fortune of the Hohenzollern family and the various claims to it. After Prince Wolrad von Schaumburg-Lippe emphatically agreed to his taking this honourable 'side job', Plettenberg accepted the office and at the same time saw to it that his friend Carl-Hans von Hardenberg was appointed as his successor and replacement.

Chapter 8

Infantry Regiment 9

In March 1939 German troops invaded the 'Rump of Czechoslovakia' and established the Protectorate of Bohemia and Moravia. At the same time Hitler demanded the integration of the free city of Danzig (now Gdansk) into Germany and the opening of an exterritorial link between East Prussia and the Reich through Polish territory, which the Polish government firmly refused. Tensions between Berlin and Warsaw thus increased significantly. The Poles made it clear that they would regard any unilateral territorial adjustment as a cause for war, and deployed troops to prevent any surprise German occupation of Danzig. In the Foreign Office in Berlin, where – in contrast to the attitude of the Hitler's loyal Foreign Minister Joachim von Ribbentrop – many civil servants still hoped for a negotiated settlement, desperate last-minute efforts were made by some diplomats, among them Ulrich von Hassel, to avoid war. Despite the guarantee given to Poland by Britain and France in case of a German attack, Hitler did not believe that the Western Powers would actually intervene and ignored all warnings from the Foreign Office, as he had done in previous crises.

In May/June 1939 Kurt von Plettenberg completed a routine reserve training exercise, and on 26 August, a few days before the outbreak of war, he was called up for service in the Wehrmacht. He had no idea that the war would separate him from his family in Bückeburg for more than two years.

Despite having shown willingness to oppose Hitler's plans for war at a meeting of the commanding generals in 1938, the supreme army commander von Brauchitsch accepted Hitler's decision to attack Poland, as did the entire General Staff. The Reich's alliance with Italy, the so-called 'Pact of Steel' of May 1939, was surprisingly followed by the conclusion of a non-aggression pact with the Soviet Union on 23 August (the 'Molotov-Ribbentrop Pact'), the secret supplementary protocol of which set out the powers' spheres of influence in Eastern Europe and agreed the division of Poland between them. Hitler believed that by this agreement he had avoided the threat of a war on two fronts, and the invasion of Poland duly began on 1 September 1939, the Red Army attacking from the east in the middle of the month.

Plettenberg served throughout the 'Blitzkrieg' campaign in Poland (which ended on 6 October 1939), as a reserve captain in IR 9, commanded by Colonel Baron von und zu Gilsa. The regiment was part of the 23rd Division under Lieutenant-General Count Brockdorff-Ahlefeldt, a friend of Plettenberg's. IR 9 was a Prussian regiment with a long tradition and Plettenberg's first choice, as there were many kindred spirits serving in it who made no secret of their rejection of Nazi ideology. The regiment had been founded in 1920 during the establishment of the 100,000-strong Reichswehr. Its motto was 'Semper talis' – 'Always the same' – in the tradition of the pre-1918 1st Foot Guards and back to Frederick William I's 'tall lads'. The regiment was based in Potsdam and was half-mockingly nicknamed 'Von 9' because of the particularly high proportion of noblemen in its ranks. It became part of the 23rd Division in 1935. No other regiment produced more members of the 20 July conspiracy.

Plettenberg met old comrades from the First World War, like Carl-Hans von Hardenberg, Gerd von Tresckow, and Ferdinand von Lüninck. He maintained friendships with many of the younger officers, particularly with Axel von dem Bussche, Fritz-Dietlof von der Schulenburg and Joachim von Willisen. Due to his military family tradition Ludwig von Hammerstein-Equord, Philipp von Bismarck, Ewald-Heinrich von Kleist-Schmenzin, Georg Sigismund von Oppen, Hasso von Boehmer and Friedrich

Karl Klausing were close to him. Henning von Tresckow, previously adjutant in IR 9, whom like his brother Gerd he already knew from the 1st Foot Guards, had meanwhile been transferred to the headquarters of Army Group A. In 1938 the divisional commander, Major General Walter von Brockdorff-Ahlefeld, stood ready with his troops in Potsdam to occupy Berlin during the 'September Conspiracy' under the command of Lieutenant General Erwin von Witzleben, when leading military figures wanted to arrest Hitler to prevent the outbreak of war during the Sudeten crisis. Brockdorff-Ahlefeld had already asked Plettenberg to join his staff in 1938. Plettenberg's immediate superior, the regimental commander Baron von und zu Gilsa, with who he was on first-name terms, was likewise not known as a Nazi sympathiser.

In retrospect Wolf Count Baudissin believed that the famous evenings in the officers' mess of IR 9 were the seed for the resistance. The unconditional bond of trust between the officers made the conspiracy possible in the first place. Even the generals who refused to take part did not denounce their comrades. Family ties in particular helped to safeguard against informers. So the will to resist slowly developed within the IR 9. There were contacts with kindred spirits in other regiments, civil departments in the Foreign Office, counterintelligence and other senior civil servants.

Criticism of the 'Browns' was the daily fare in the regiment. Axel von dem Bussche later recalled how disrespectfully they spoke about Hitler: 'We did not speak of him as the Führer. For us he was always merely Adolf.' According to the unwritten law of the mess, none of this ever got out. Even for pro-Nazi officers, esprit de corps trumped political convictions.

Hans Frank, Minister of Justice under Hitler and head of the legal department of the NSDAP, served as lieutenant of the reserve in IR 9 until his appointment as Governor-General of Poland. Shortly before his execution in 1946 he gave this vivid account of the tone in the officers' mess.

Hitler was highly respected in this circle, solely because of his restoration of the Wehrmacht, but not loved. The old guard were alarmed by his liability to disaster and there was general disagreement with the aggressiveness of the noisy tone of Goebbels, the buffoonery of Göring, and the brutality of Himmler and Heydrich. This was anything but 'Prussian' … None of these officers understood the anti-Semitism of the specific 'Nazi' kind which they declared insane … I for my part found these Potsdam men to be splendid fellows, who picked the Third Reich to pieces, but still fulfilled their duty to the state and also to Hitler as eagerly and successfully as for everybody else in their history.

A telling episode recorded by Mainhardt Count Nayhauß illuminates the esprit de corps within the regiment. In June 1943 Richard von Weizsäcker, together with the 24-year-old Axel von dem Bussche and the 23-year-old Friedrich Karl Klausing, were at the siege of Leningrad a few kilometres from Zarskoje Selo. They were positioned 'at the Neva River and south of Lake Ladoga. The regiment lost 618 of 843 men in this period – fallen, wounded, taken prisoner or missing.' During a dinner in a confiscated dacha alcohol spurred the young senior lieutenant Hans Albrecht Bronsart von Schellendorf 'in the absence of the host to fire a bullet into a portrait of Hitler on the wall; first laughter, then awkward silence. What would happen the next day when the regimental commander discovered the bullet hole? Richard von Weizsäcker was the first to speak. 'Before we agree on what to do, everyone has to shoot at the picture.' No sooner he had said this, then he drew his weapon and fired. And so it happened. Richard von Weizsäcker shot a second hole in the portrait of the Führer; Axel and the remaining three comrades followed his example. Besides Schellendorf these were Bussche, Klausing, Kleist, Quadt, Arnim, and Weizsäcker. Only one did not shoot.

Later they pretended to beat up the regiment commander, as Axel von dem Bussche recounted after the war. 'He did not enjoy great authority and had no sense of humour', wrote Richard von

Weizsäcker to Plettenberg's son in 2002. The commander could not report the incident under any circumstances, otherwise he would have been relieved of command due to lack of authority over his subordinates. It was out of the question that such incidents became known outside the regiment.

IR 9's campaign in Poland, as Plettenberg must have experienced it, can be reconstructed from the memoirs of his fellow officers and Wehrmacht situation reports. On the night of 1 September 1939 the regiment crossed the Polish border from the Groß Born military training area near Neustettin. Its c.3,000 men followed Guderian's panzer corps which formed the spearhead of the invasion. When the tanks got into the first heavy fighting with Polish troops, the 23rd Division moved up to break any resistance. During the fighting in Bory Tucholskie near Klonowo, south-west of Gdansk, the first fallen comrades had to mourned, among them Heinrich von Weizsäcker, Richard's older brother.

On 6 September the regiment received a brief personal visit from Hitler who congratulated them on their successes. By this time Britain and France had already declared war on the German Reich, but without being able to directly support Poland militarily.

Infantry Regiment 9 continued its advance along the Vistula without encountering serious Polish resistance, crossed the river near Gniew and reached East Prussia from where it was moved by train to E□k. Resuming their march there, they crossed the Narew with the help of German air support to finally reach Bialystok on 17 September. A few days later the town was handed over to the Red Army by two officers of IR 9 according to the Molotov-Ribbentrop Pact. They were Hermann Jannsen and Constantin von Quadt, a distant cousin of Plettenberg who would marry the widowed Arianne von Plettenberg in 1954.

The regiment only suffered minor losses after a march of 470km. Even so, on the day of the handover of Bialystok the division received orders to march back to East Prussia. From Straduny they travelled by train to Königsberg and from there by ship to Szczecin.

* * *

Plettenberg's diaries for the Polish campaign have not survived, but we can assume that his experiences were similar to those which his comrade, and later friend, Axel von dem Bussche described after the war.

In 1939 after a battle near the Vistula Bussche encountered a lieutenant of the military police attached to a unit assigned to 'mopping-up' who had rounded up thirty young people. After hearing gunfire from behind the local cemetery, Bussche asked the lieutenant what he had done. The lieutenant replied: 'I have had half of those young people shot because they were Poles. They had fired upon German troops.' The lieutenant has determined who was Polish by asking if they were Catholics: 'The others were ethnic Germans.' Furious, Bussche reports the incident to his superiors. A madman was having Catholics shot. However, at this stage he still believed that this was an isolated incident.

Bussche also told how in November 1940, while stationed as the occupying troops in a town in southern East Prussia, he, Plettenberg and the other officers were in a 'helpless and desolate mood' having witnessed the first excesses against the Jews carried out by the German civil administration. 'At that time open discussions began in the mess. How could things have gone so far? What can and must we do?'

Plettenberg and Bussche learnt more about the murderous actions of the *Einsatzgruppen* behind the line from Fritz-Dietlof von der Schulenburg. Later, Plettenberg's friend Hardenberg must also have told him about the terrible events in Borissow in October 1941, where 7,000 Jews were murdered. 'He [Hardenberg] had flown over the town in low altitude during the "action" and had seen how a Latvian SS unit rounded up the inhabitants of the ghetto, some several thousand Jews, and murdered them.'

In the winter of 1940/41, when the regiment was stationed in the Poznan region in preparation for the Russian campaign, Bussche witnessed how Jews in the small town of Wloclawek were driven with whips into a ghetto in front of a jeering crowd.

He reported the incident to his commanding officer, Colonel Gilsa:

> 'This is a scandal!', the commander shouted furiously. 'Which idiot dreamt up something like that! Tomorrow morning I will drive to Cracow to Frank and tell him everything.' [He knew Frank from the Olympic Games in Berlin where the latter had been in charge of the Olympic Village.) The next morning the car was made ready, but before departure the adjutant [Bussche] said: 'Yet what if that was no idiot? What if that … is German policy?' – 'You think so?' von und zu Gilsa replied irresolutely and let the car be driven back into the garage.

In autumn 1942 Axel von dem Bussche was stationed in the Ukraine west of the Dnepr River in a town called Dubno. During one of his rides in the countryside he witnessed mass shootings.

> He already knew the pit. Naked people stood in front of the pit, men, women, the aged and children. They stood lined up in a perfectly regular queue, like lining up for milk and bread. The queue was around 600 metres long. At the edge of the pit sat a SS man. He let his legs dangle and held a machine gun in his hands. He gave a sign, and the queue started to move forward. The people climbed down the steps dug into the earth and laid down in the pit, one next to the other, face down. The SS man fired, immediately waved again and the queue moved forward. … Naked women carried naked toddlers. Men led children by the hand or supported faltering old people. Families stood embraced. Nobody was screaming or crying, nobody was praying or begging for mercy, and nobody tried to flee. Between the shots total silence prevailed. There were eight SS men … The operation at the airport lasted two days, and three thousand people were shot.

In January 1943 Axel von dem Bussche decided to kill Hitler. He would volunteer as an assassin in the resistance. The massacres and other atrocities are seen by many officers and men as a disgraceful besmirching of the honour of the army, although only a few protest openly at the beginning. In the course of the Polish campaign the murderous acts against the Jewish and Polish population behind the front by SS *Einsatzgruppen* and police battalions made the regime's policy of extermination so obvious that finally officers began to make complaints to their superiors. General Johannes Blaskowitz, the supreme commander in the East, protested against these actions in two memoranda to the supreme army command. In one of them he wrote: 'The attitude of the troop towards the SS and police is one of revulsion and hate. Each soldier is disgusted and repelled by these crimes which are committed in Poland by members of the Reich and representatives of the state.'

The protests were unsuccessful, for after talks with Himmler, in a statement dated 7 February 1940 about the 'army and SS' Brauchitsch expressed understanding for the 'necessary solution order by the leaders … of ethnic policy, [which] inevitably have to lead to otherwise unusually severe measures against the Polish population'. For a long time prudent commanders tried to keep the army away from the terrible murder campaigns as far as possible, but as the war continued this became increasingly difficult. With the help of the counterintelligence agent Helmuth Groscurth, Blaskowitz's reports also reached the army commanders in the West, without having any great effect, however. On Hitler's orders Blaskowitz was relieved of his command in Poland in May 1940 and later transferred to the Western Front.

Shortly before the end of the Polish campaign, in September 1940, IR 9 was transferred to the Western Front. The French had retreated behind the Maginot Line and the German units are ordered to secure the border on the German side. Regimental headquarters was on the border with Luxembourg, north-west of Bitburg in the Eifel, in part of the Siegfried Line. As divisional adjutant (IIa), Plettenberg was busy with personnel administration, work which did not fulfil him.

The next seven months were the so-called 'Phoney War'. Plettenberg's friend, the forester Joachim von Willisen, recalls icy winter days and a Christmas celebration in Nittel at the Upper Moselle. During this unusually severe winter the troops' was maintained through training and exercises with new weapons. The division had already received the detailed deployment orders for the attack next spring.

Plettenberg's attitude to the war had already been expressed in a letter to his cousin Elisabeth dated 3 November 1939:

> You can imagine how much I suffer because of all this. According to my attitude I am probably indeed a 'pacifist' and in Poland I have suffered because of the unabated terror of war perhaps even more than 25 years ago.
>
> I also fear the future disasters of humanity. Yet I <u>cannot</u> stand aside, when the young German squad is fighting. The only thing providing comfort in such times is the loyalty and courage of the young soldiers and that helps in seeing it through. ...
>
> And if – it cannot be denied that the chances for this are very great – I do not return home, please remain friends with my dear little wife and tell her sometimes of you and me. I have lost my heart so entirely to her natural, gracefully feminine manner that this war is so infinitely more difficult to me than the previous one. Not so much for my sake as for that of my wife and children. Yet what am I to do? I <u>cannot</u> stand aside ...

Plettenberg was offered a transfer to the forestry administration in occupied Poland in October 1939, but he refused, writing: 'I have answered – as long as battles at the Western Front are to be expected – that I would not be willing to transfer to the forest administration.'

In February 1940 Lieutenant-General Count Brockdorff-Ahlefeldt wanted Plettenberg as adjutant of 1st Division. Plettenberg held the general in great esteem and felt politically close to him, but on 26 February he wrote to his wife Arianne: 'As long as I have been a soldier, I have been incessantly pursued by assaults of higher staff who wanted to pull me in. Again and again I have fended these off and thought to have put the record straight this time by the course I have taken.' Plettenberg, who was much more suited to troop leadership than to the staff, remained with his men for the time being.

In spring 1940 the peaceful bivouac came to an end. After the occupation of Norway and Denmark in March, Hitler ordered the invasion of neutral Belgium, Luxembourg and the Netherlands. On 10 May the division, numbering over 18,000 men and 5,000 horses, crossed the territory of Luxembourg without resistance, heading for southern Belgium where the first fighting took place. Their objective then became Charleville on the Meuse, the French border. The French bunkers defending the bridge were overrun in a surprise attack and the bridge itself captured intact. On 16 May the 23rd Division broke through the Maginot Line. In accordance with Operation 'Sickle Cut' it then turned south to secure the flank of the tank units, and after heavy fighting and considerable losses forced the crossing over the Aisne near Asfeld-la-Ville. Long marches through the Champagne battlefields, which Plettenberg knew from the First World War, followed. Battles for the Rhine-Marne Canal and the crossing of the Marne near St. Dizier brought the division into the centre of Burgundy near Dijon on 19 June. The objective was the Le Creusot armament factories. After France's capitulation on 22 June the division was ordered to secure the demarcation line on the Franco-Swiss border near Montbéliard.

After this Plettenberg's wish for battalion command was finally fulfilled. On 3 July 1940 he took over the 3rd Battalion of IR 9 as major of the reserve in the 23rd Division under Colonel Baron von und zu Gilsa. After three months this battalion was transferred to the newly-formed 123rd Division under General Walter Lichel and moved to East Prussia.

Plettenberg remained in command of his battalion until the end of February 1941. Apart from some short leaves and a battalion commanders' course, he had been on active service for seventeen months, so he requested a working leave of three months to attend to business at the court chamber of Schaumburg-Lippe, which was granted. But afterwards he was refused command of a battalion again by Major General Hellmich, without any reason being given, despite assurances from the division by telegram. Plettenberg had anticipated such difficulties and in February 1941 had already asked his old regimental comrade and friend Henning von Tresckow for his support, as he would need his help 'perhaps in May, when there is no free battalion at Semper Talis, because I could not tolerate a summer at home.'

In a letter to Hellmich dated 10 April 1941 he tried to apply pressure by saying that he had rejected 'a request of Field Marshal von Bock, who wished to ask for me for special duties and made an early enquiry through Lieutenant Colonel von Tresckow, because I am of the opinion that for me the leaving of my work in my civilian profession cannot be readily justified by being in service at any higher staff, but only by contributing to the war effort of the troops in a responsible post.'

It was futile. Hellmich, a staunch National Socialist, could not be persuaded. Even telegrams to the regiment commander Jonas Count Eulenburg, asking General Walter Lichel to intervene on his behalf with Hellmich, were of no help in the end. On 8 May Plettenberg had to take over the replacement battalion of the IR 9 in Potsdam. One last time, he asked in Berlin to be allowed to lead a battalion in the field but was told that there were no vacant posts. He stayed in Potsdam for two months, followed by a brief leave in Bückeburg at the beginning of July 1941.

After the beginning of the Russian campaign, on 24 June 1941, he was finally recalled to the Eastern Front on 5 July 1941, where he took command of the 3rd Battalion of IR 415, a sister regiment of IR 9. From East Prussia they advanced to Sebezh and Demyansk in northern Russia and were drawn into heavy fighting in the Valdai Hills. From 8 October to 22 November 1941 Kurt von Plettenberg was in command of IR 415 as a whole.

The war reporter Werner Siegel portrayed Kurt von Plettenberg in November under the title: *The Invulnerable Heart – Portrait of a Major.* This shows, nevertheless, how highly Plettenberg was regarded by his soldiers because of his courage and personal commitment. Spiegel reported of the advance:

> When the battalion in its attack against D. came to the abatis, the major ordered a halt and said to the advance guard that it was presumably mined. Then he went towards it, found a narrow, just shoulder-wide gap in the brushwood at the side, and went through it, followed by the officers of his battalion staff. When they had left it behind, he ordered to cautiously move on through the gap. The entire battalion passed through in this manner – the pioneers at the battalion's heels found there next to the footprints a large box full of carefully hidden, devilishly fixed explosives whose camouflaged lanyards would have responded to the slightest pull. Yet let us repeat in more detail what the major said in the moment when he ordered the halt. He said: 'I am afraid that here are mines!' Then he went first …

The troops had to defend themselves on all sides, and Plettenberg moved from position to position, upright and without fear, 'as if there was no shooting', as one soldier put it. But Plettenberg was not invulnerable.

> Four days ago the Soviets put a grenade right in at his feet … A splinter hit his leg. The report of his injury spread like wildfire through the battalion and the telephone at the command post was seeing heavy use, as everybody wanted to hear again that the injury was not bad and if the commander could stay with the unit. Yet it can be said for certain that the battalion's men did not hanker for the phone out of dismay that their belief in their major's invulnerability had been wrecked, but out of fond concern …

On 4 October 1941 Plettenberg was wounded by a grenade splinter. He received the Wound Badge on 15 November. The months from July to November 1941 were the most intensive part of his wartime career. His commitment was also recognised by the highest authorities: on 9 January 1942 he received the German Cross in Gold, which was awarded for 'frequently demonstrated extraordinary bravery or for frequent outstanding services in troop leadership'. Axel von dem Bussche explained: 'This was a new decoration. It assumed that one had demonstrably fulfilled five times the conditions for the Iron Cross First Class – on separate occasions.' Plettenberg never wore this medal. Quite fittingly, the soldiers called it 'The Fried Egg with Swastika'.

Chapter 9

In the Service of the Hohenzollerns

As early as January 1940, while Plettenberg was serving on the staff of the 23rd Division which was guarding the German western border against a potential attack by French troops, General von Dommes, the general agent of the house of Hohenzollern, attempted to recruit Plettenberg as his successor. Prince Wolrad von Schaumburg-Lippe received a personal letter from the Crown Prince in which the latter asked him to release Plettenberg for the soon-to-be-vacant position:

> ... after he has completed the great tasks which you have given him regarding your estate, I still hope that a way will be found to fulfil my wish to see Plettenberg at the head of my administration.
>
> Now I have asked Plettenberg to take on as a side job a consulting supervision over the enterprises of the court chamber while we have no president for the court chamber – the position will remain vacant for now. Plettenberg wants to oblige, provided he has your permission.

Prince Wolrad felt unable to agree to the Crown Prince's request given the extremely difficult position his estate had been in since the hyper-inflation and the abolition of entails, and particularly in the middle of a war. He replied:

I write this to you only to show you that my administration is a difficult task for which special skill is required. Therefore it took me roughly a year to find a gentleman of whom I could expect that he is the right man. Among the many gentlemen applying for the post I did not find one I really considered capable to fill it with its multifaceted demands. It is now particularly pleasant for me that apart from his efficiency, Plettenberg is a born Bückeburgian, known to me from childhood and in addition a regimental comrade from the world war to whom I feel bound in friendship.

Plettenberg himself – after learning of the exchange of letters between the Crown Prince and Prince Wolrad – answers the honourable request negatively. Shortly after he communicated his reasons to Dommes:

I have told His Imperial Highness that because of the upcoming war I could not accept the offer, nor the one from the Reich Forestry Office here on the instigation of Prince Schaumburg-Lippe. It would seem wrong to me to practically miss this event which in all probability will really decide the fate of the fatherland. Thus I must remain a soldier for now. As long as the war lasts or as long as I am fit enough to participate in it as an active soldier, the question of my future occupation moves actually somewhat into the background, because there is no guarantee if afterwards I will still be here or able to take on such work.

Also, Plettenberg added that at that critical time he could not 'betray' his current employer, Prince Schaumburg-Lippe. However, he was not adverse in principle to taking up the new challenge posed by an administration of such size at some point in the future. After his death in June 1941, the estate of Emperor Wilhelm II was estimated at 70 to 80 million Reichsmarks. Therefore, he wrote to Dommes in March 1940:

> I will not deny that I am very much interested in this administration. For me there are more traditional reasons than practical or material ones, for my life would be certainly more pleasant and equally interesting here. Therefore I have explained to the crown prince in agreement with the prince that I could not make any decision at all during the war and only could take over his administration, when I have managed to create complete order here.

At the end of 1941 Plettenberg was in Bückeburg again and after all preparing to take over the management of the Hohenzollerns' assets. General von Dommes had not given up in his efforts to entice him away from the house of Schaumburg-Lippe. An initial private conversation between the Crown Prince and Prince Wolrad in July 1941 at Glienicke Castle near Berlin brought no result. Yet the Hohenzollerns finally managed to bring Prince Wolrad around. What motivated Plettenberg himself to give in to the Crown Prince's wishes cannot be determined from the documents. Perhaps it was the challenge of the demanding new job.

Dommes could now confirm, in a letter dated 31 December 1941, that the Crown Prince had appointed Kurt von Plettenberg as his 'general agent' and had conferred on him the directorship of the administration of the Prussian royal house from 1 January 1942. The office of president of the court chamber of Schaumburg-Lippe in Bückeburg would be retained by Plettenberg 'on the basis of the conditions agreed'. His office as general agent for the Hohenzollerns will be in Berlin, but the office of the court chamber president of Schaumburg-Lippe, as well as his family home, remained in Bückeburg, meaning that a lot of exhausting travel became unavoidable.

At that time the Hohenzollern administration was divided into five main departments: affairs of the members of the royal house, administration of the foundation, the business of the Crown Prince, asset management and real estate management. The last was directly under Plettenberg's control. Plettenberg's deputies are the Crown Prince's chief of cabinet, Ludwig Müldner von Mülnheim, and privy councillor Arthur Berg.

After leave of absence from the Wehrmacht, beginning on 22 November 1941, Plettenberg officially took up his new office on 1 January 1942. On 9 January the crown prince asked III Army Corps to defer Plettenberg from military service or to grant an extension of his leave for half a year. He justified this by 'the great economic success of the management by Kurt von Plettenberg' which made him indispensable to the 300,000-acre estate. On 28 January 1942 the Crown Prince grants his court chamber president full power of attorney in all matters.

Plettenberg reported the change on 27 January to the district headquarters in Hameln. To avoid any appearance of shirking, he added:

> When I made my application for a longer leave of absence, my divisional commander as well as the commanding general were of the opinion that the division, which until then had seen very many heavy battles and was positioned in the lakeland area of Valday, would be looking at a longer period of rest. Had I been able to foresee at that time how the situation on the Eastern Front would develop, I would naturally not have made my application for leave. Thus I am in a very difficult situation, because on 1st January I have taken over the general administration of the former royal house of Hohenzollern in addition to my service in Bückeburg. After the previous general agent retired on 1st January, it is now of course rather difficult to remove myself again from this sphere of activity, though I consider this necessary in April at the latest.

He never returned to the division. On 25 March Plettenberg was transferred to Infantry Replacement Battalion 338 at Crossen/Oder, the replacement unit of IR 415, without having to report. On 3 May 1942 his permanent dismissal from military service followed. Active service was thus now even officially over for him. He found it difficult to adapt to these new circumstances of a civilian occupation in wartime. In June 1942 he wrote to his cousin Elisabeth:

> I have an infinite amount of work, but I will manage somehow. It is worse that I cannot be with the soldiers. For eight summers I was a soldier – 14, 15, 16, 17, 18, 39, 40, 41, then two summers of mobile warfare, and now I am sitting at home, at the peak of my ability. I can only stomach this with difficulty.

In Berlin, Plettenberg had his office at first in the Dutch Palace, Unter den Linden 11, next to the Crown Prince's palace. In the Dutch Palace, the Crown Prince maintained an apartment on the first floor which was temporarily also inhabited by Hermine, Emperor Wilhelm's widow. Plettenberg moved into a suite of offices and private rooms on the floor above. However, the palace was so badly damaged during the devastating bombing raid on the centre of Berlin on the night of 23 November 1943 that it became almost uninhabitable.

Axel von dem Bussche and his boyhood friend Konrad von der Groeben were Plettenberg's guests that evening. After the war they told his son Karl-Wilhelm what happened. Bussche:

> Your father immediately took over the organisation of the rescue efforts. Karl Konrad Groeben was told to get the emperor's widow Hermine, who had fled from the crown prince's apartment into the basement, out of the building. To me he [Plettenberg] said: 'Axel, you will now receive the order many Germans would have liked to carry out a long time ago. You have to clear out the crown prince's room!' I went into the room on the first floor, sat down in a corner and thought about how best to begin. On tables and dressers stood many precious items, especially numerous silver-framed photos of beautiful women and of his relatives. While I was still considering the matter, the chandelier suddenly fell

from the ceiling with a tremendous crash. In great haste and without further ado I ripped the curtains from the rails. Some had already caught fire and I threw them out of the window. Into the other curtains I threw whatever I could grab from the tables, trunks and wardrobes, tied them up and let them drop from the window onto the pavement of Unter den Linden.

Groeben added:

I accompanied the emperor's widow Hermine across the street and settled the old lady on a large pile of duvets and cushions on the pavement in front of the arsenal. Later I took her down to its basement. For the first time of my life I experienced the almost unbelievable winds generated by the firestorm. These were so strong that they ripped the canvasses from the heavy picture frames on Unter den Linden, which I carried to the other side of the street to the arsenal.

A few days later Axel von dem Bussche travelled by train to Mauerwald to prepare for the planned assassination of Hitler. After the raid Kurt von Plettenberg described the situation in Berlin in a letter to Marion Dönhoff:

Cecilienhof, 11th December 1943
In Berlin we have had four great raids which have changed the appearance of the city drastically. The west is destroyed – from Potsdamer Platz to western Charlottenburg, Tiergartenstraße and the area from Hofjägerallee to the Zoo including the latter, likewise Berliner Straße to Charlottenburg Castle completely. I do not know about the east. In the west, centre and south I estimate the damage at 20 per cent. For us, the court chamber in Charlottenburg and the Emperor Wilhelm's Palace are completely devastated. My pretty house and our large furniture store are half destroyed. … At the moment I am living in Cecilienhof.

Plettenberg's office was relocated to Potsdam which had been spared bombing thus far, namely to the Crown Prince's castle of Cecilienhof at Heiligen See, where he obtained a room as makeshift accommodation in a side wing, the so-called Nun's Walk.

His family spent the entire war in rural Bückeburg, largely spared any bombing. In October 1943 his third child was born there, his daughter Dorothea-Marion. Among her twelve godparents were Marion Dönhoff, the Crown Prince and Prince Wolrad. To a friend, a Hamburg lawyer mourning the death and severe injury of two sons, Plettenberg wrote in January 1944 full of foreboding:

> My three children are – I am tempted to thank God – still little and are at least not yet seized immediately by war and military duty. What the future of the homeland will be, however, and what circumstances these children will find one day nobody knows. At any rate they will probably differ very greatly from ours.

Chapter 10

Inside the Resistance Network

The first opposition from high-ranking officers to Hitler's plans for war arose around the turn of the year 1937/38. In particular, the War Minister Werner von Blomberg and the commander-in-chief of the army Werner von Fritsch provoked Hitler's anger by their criticism of his policies. Thanks to false allegations of homosexuality against Fritsch, spread by the SS and the Gestapo, and Blomberg's marriage to a woman who turned out to be a former prostitute, Hitler was able to remove them from office.

The removal of Fritsch deeply disturbed many officers including Plettenberg, Fritsch being his first uncle once removed. At the end of 1938, Ludwig Beck noted in his diary: 'Fritsch's case has opened a rift between leader and the Wehrmacht's officer corps ... which can never again be bridged.'

Soon after, the efforts to rehabilitate Fritsch united different forces within the army and counterintelligence. There were discussions as to how the power of the SS could be broken and the position of the armed forces relative to the Party strengthened. However, this did not mean there was as yet disagreement in principle with Hitler's overall political aims. The national conservative opposition within the military and diplomatic service also wanted the revision of the Treaty of Versailles and the reestablishment of the German Reich as a European superpower under an authoritarian government. They did not rule out the use of military force to assert these aims. 'Opposition and cooperation' (Klaus-Jürgen Müller) defined their attitude towards the Führer and his policies.

The officers saw it as their duty to serve as soldiers for the Fatherland and carried out that duty in accordance with their own code of conduct. This made disobedience to the supreme commander very difficult, as did the duty of obedience to the state authorities ordained of God (Romans 13,1-2) which was part of the Prussian-Protestant tradition in which these men had been raised.

It was not until the Sudeten Crisis of 1938, when Hitler made it known that he sought the break-up of Czechoslovakia as soon as possible, that an 'anti-war party' directly aimed against Hitler was formed, headed by the Chief of the General Staff Ludwig Beck, his deputy Franz Halder and the head of the counterintelligence service Admiral Wilhelm Canaris. They feared that Hitler's plans would trigger a general European war which Germany would not be able to win especially since, unlike Hitler, they did not believe that Great Britain would remain neutral.

Initially, Beck had tried to persuade Hitler to change his plans, and when this failed he tried to prompt the generals to resign en masse, but this was also unsuccessful. Beck then planned a move by the military against the 'radical forces' in the Party and the SS which supported Hitler's plans for war. He attempted to get the commander-in-chief of the army, General Walter von Brauchitsch, to agree to refuse any order by Hitler to go to war, and also to demand a clarification of the relationship between the Wehrmacht and the SS in order to 'restore justice within the Reich'.

The 'September Conspiracy' of 1938 which should have prevented the outbreak of war at the last moment – Hitler had originally announced 28 September as the date for mobilisation – relied Erwin von Witzleben, the commander of Military District III/Berlin, and the president of the Berlin police, Wolf-Heinrich Graf von Helldorf, who were both opponents of the regime. Yet Beck did not manage to get Brauchitsch to take a firm stance against Hitler. Therefore, he resigned as Chief of the General Staff on 18 August 1938, especially since he had failed to establish the General Staff as the sole advisory body to the Führer in matters of national defence.

His successor Franz Halder at first continued the preparations for the coup together with Canaris. The group around the counterintelligence officer Hans Oster also decided, together with General von Witzleben, to arrest Hitler at an appropriate opportunity. Yet the signing of the Munich agreement on 29 September 1938 stymied them. With this Hitler had been able to achieve his Sudeten German plans without having to fear a declaration of war by the major powers. Since the immediate threat of war seemed to be over, and Hitler had achieved a 'great success', the conspirators feared that the military elite and the wider population would not support a *coup d'état* – a fear that would haunt the resistance from then onwards.

As a result of the abortive uprising a feeling of impotence and resignation spread among the plotters. Halder did not want to try again until Hitler had suffered some sort of setback. It was not until Hitler began to prepare for war with Poland that the opposition became active again. After the Germans had moved into the rump of Czechoslovakia in March 1939, Great Britain and France had issued a guarantee to Poland following Hitler's demands for the return of Danzig and the creation of a 'corridor' to East Prussia. '.

Through diplomatic emissaries, among them Adam von Trott zu Solz, who had established contact with the British Foreign Office, the opposition sought to encourage the Western Powers to take a firm stance against Hitler. The circle around Oster, Beck, Goerdeler, Hassell and Popitz simultaneously attempted to influence Hitler with the help of middlemen close to him.

Yet the rapid success of the 'Blitzkrieg' against Poland once again paralysed the opposition. Only when Hitler scheduled the attack on France for 12 November 1939, did vehement protests arise once more among parts of the military leadership, who feared a war on two fronts and did not consider the German Reich sufficiently prepared for this situation. Halder acceded to the demands of the active opposition and laid plans for a coup to overthrow the regime as a whole, not just prevent the war in the West. Oster and Groscurth sounded out the commanders in the West and made contact with the civilian conservative opposition. Explosives for the assassination of Hitler were obtained and plans made for the occupation of key points under a state of emergency to deprive the Party and the SS of their power.

Before the *coup d'état* Brauchitsch was to make it plain to Hitler on 5 November 1939 that the entire army command rejected the Western offensive. Yet at the decisive moment the general did not stand up to the Führer. Hitler's angry outburst at Brauchitsch did the job. When the he threatened to destroy the 'spirit of Zossen' – the headquarters of the General Staff there – and thus directly attacked the generals opposing his war plans, Brauchitsch erroneously presumed that the conspiracy had been discovered. Immediately he had all documents destroyed and afterwards refused all further preparations for a *coup d'état*.

Actually Hitler postponed the order to attack on the Western Front several times, until the summer of 1940. Halder now withdrew completely from the conspiracy. Groscurth, who had worked tirelessly for the uprising, spoke for many of his fellow conspirators: 'These undecided leaders disgust me. Horrid.' Ulrich von Hassell noted in his diary: 'According to his [Goederler's] account any opposition of the military leadership to the march through [Belgium] has broken down, although like everyone else Brauchitsch and Halder are convinced of its disastrous effect. Yet they are of the opinion that they have to obey.' Until the attack on France on 5 June 1940 only occasional diplomatic actions by the opposition took place, as they once more attempted in vain to prevent the worst through their contacts abroad. The occupation of Denmark and Norway, the unopposed march through Belgium, the capitulation of the Netherlands and the armistice with France in the forest of Compiègne on 22 June 1940, by which the humiliation of Versailles was blotted out, saw Hitler at the height of his power. Nothing seemed to be able to prevent his rise to supremacy over Europe. His support both in the population and in the army meant that most of the military leaders who had favoured his removal gave up. They were no longer approachable by the resistance.

Renewed resistance emerged, however, in December 1940 when Hitler gave orders to plan an attack on the Soviet Union and gave the start date for Operation *Barbarossa* as May 1941, This time new, younger elements within the military took the lead in plotting Hitler's removal. For them it was clear Hitler had first to be deposed or eliminated so that the military leadership would be freed of it oath to the Führer.

At this point it should be appreciated that a war against 'Bolshevism' was popular among many military leaders and the Wehrmacht's hitherto unprecedented run of successes did much to silence concerns about further expansion of the war. For these reasons, the 'Commissar Order' by which the murder of Soviet political officers was 'legalised', thus met only little opposition. Since this was against both international and military law, in the eyes of many it sealed the moral bankruptcy of the Wehrmacht. Ulrich von Hassell lamented in his diary in May 1941: 'With this submission to Hitler's orders Br[auchitsch] sacrifices the honour of the German army.'

Only Field Marshal Fedor von Bock, pressured forcefully by his chief of the staff Henning von Tresckow, registered his protest against this order with Hitler. Tresckow, a veteran of IR 9, became the head of a new faction of officers working on definite plans for Hitler's removal, even at the risk of their own lives. From the Eastern Front Tresckow created a resistance network and made contact with the Berlin centre of opposition around Colonel-General Ludwig Beck, Hans Oster and Carl Goerdeler. He came to an understanding with confidants in the Army Office at Bendlerstraße, in the reserve army and the Berlin city command. With the aid of trustworthy intermediaries Tresckow also made contact with the military commander in France, Carl-Heinrich von Stülpnagel, and with Alexander von Falkenhausen in Belgium, in order to have a wider basis for the takeover of power by the military.

Beginning in the spring of 1943, Tresckow organised several attempts on Hitler's life, which were planned in detail with trustworthy officers. The assassination was supposed to be the 'initial spark' (Peter Hoffmann) for a takeover of the government by the army. In March, Hitler was supposed to be killed during a visit to the headquarters of Army Group Centre in Smolensk. During lunch, at an agreed signal young officers like von Schlabrendorff, von Voß, Eggert, von Oertzen, von Breitenbuch and others would shoot Hitler together with their pistols. However, when Field Marshal Günther von Kluge learnt of this, he forbade it.

Afterwards, Fabian von Schlabrendorff still managed to plant a time bomb on Hitler's plane, but the detonator failed. Schlabrendorff flew to Rastenburg in East Prussia, close to Hitler's headquarters, to recover the package which contained the bomb camouflaged as a bottle of cognac. The next opportunity presented itself eight days later during the opening of an exhibition in Berlin. Rudolph-Christoph von Gersdorff intended to blow himself up together with Hitler, Göring, Himmler and others, but Hitler left the exhibition early.

After Axel von dem Bussche had declared his readiness to kill Hitler to Stauffenberg, another plan for a suicide attack in December 1943 was developed. Bussche wanted to kill himself together with Hitler during the presentation of new Wehrmacht uniforms in which explosives would be hidden, but the event had to be cancelled, as the uniforms were destroyed in an Allied bombing raid. Also during a later presentation in February 1944 the attack on Hitler by Ewald Heinrich von Kleist failed, because the event was cancelled at short notice. Finally Eberhard von Breitenbruch, recruited by Tresckow, failed in his attempt to shoot Hitler at the Berghof with his pistol, because adjutants were not admitted to the Führer conference.

While these attempts were being made, Tresckow and Claus Schenk Count von Stauffenberg of the General Staff began the planning for Operation *Valkyrie* with the head of the General Army Office, General Friedrich Olbricht, and his assistant Colonel

Albrecht Baronet Mertz von Quirnheim, which would result in the assassination attempt of 20 July 1944.

Parallel to these assassination attempts Tresckow and the officers of the General Staff had begun in July 1943 to plan 'Operation *Valkyrie*' which would lead to the attempt of 20 July 1944. The conspirators' efforts were received ambivalently by the military leaders. Carl-Hans von Hardenberg later recalled:

> Already the first meetings we had with the individual field marshals and colonel-generals had shown that not a single one of them was willing to step in against us. Almost all had toyed with the idea, accepted its necessity, and expressed their willingness to join in against Hitler, if someone else took on the responsibility … When the operation progressed, it became clear that indeed the military leaders were not willing to intervene against us, but also that only a few, like Witzleben, Beck, Hoepner, Rommel and Stülpnagel, were ready to commit themselves personally. Again and again, since autumn 1943, plans were developed and dates set, but the tyranny was exercised so rigorously that it was not possible to act for a long time … The more the circle widened beyond the closest associates, the more the danger of betrayal increased, less from evil intentions than rather due to unfortunate loquacity and vanity. If nevertheless the Gestapo could not intervene, it was only due to the fact that everyone was worried to put the noose around their necks.

* * *

After Kurt von Plettenberg's return to Berlin from the Eastern Front at the beginning of 1942 he maintained close contact with the conspirators from his office in the Dutch Palace. As already mentioned, he had been friends with some of them for many years, for example Carl-Hans von Hardenberg, Henning von Tresckow, Kurt von Hammerstein, the ambassador Friedrich-Werner von der Schulenburg and his relative Fritz-Dietlof von der Schulenburg. To others of the resistance his contacts intensified in the circle of IR 9 as the war continued. Long-standing family relationships helped in the building of trust. They socialised regularly in Berlin and Potsdam, exchanged information with visitors and conspired during seemingly innocent family gatherings.

Plettenberg not only maintained contacts with the military, but also the civilian groups of the resistance and acted as a highly-valued intermediary between them. Not only via Fritz-Dietlof von der Schulenburg, but also personally he was in contact with the Kreisau Circle. Peter Yorck von Wartenburg mentioned him in a letter to his mother: 'He is an especially congenial and clever person, and it is certainly good that the Hohenzollerns have acquired him. How sad that this house seems so burnt out and has no pretender to the crown … What effect would such a personage have in these times.'

Plettenberg also met several times with the editor of the *Weiße Blätter*, the Catholic conservative monarchist Karl Ludwig von und zu Guttenberg. Plettenberg kept in touch with the circle around Goerdeler via Johannes Popitz and Kunrat von Hammerstein. How far Plettenberg's contacts reached became clear to Axel von dem Bussche during the first years of the war: 'He took me along on a visit to Field Marshal von Kluge, for he knew him like most of the others, too: the ministers and secretaries of state, the ambassadors and likewise the marshals, without giving in to illusions or hopes. And he could explain the "sociology" of these great and apparently powerful men of the nation …'

Plettenberg was experienced. He had a realistic view of the regime so tried not to make himself an obvious target. Therefore, he only confided in those few people he was absolutely certain of. He avoided writing anything down. Also his colleagues in the Hohenzollern administration were not told of his conspiratorial activities. How essential for his survival this caution was becomes evident from a note in the diary of the former ambassador and member of the inner circle of the conspirators Ulrich von Hassell.

He reported from a dinner with the 'nice' Plettenberg in the Dutch Palace on 25 March 1943 at which Ulrich Schwerin von Schwanenfeld and Fritz-Dietlof von der Schulenburg (deputy police president in Berlin from 1937 to 1939) were also present. Von Hassell wrote: 'The latter told me "they" have informed him that I also would be monitored by telephone the next day, likewise Pl[ettenberg[and Prince L[ouis] F[erdinand]. I was only surprised that it was actually only happening now. Thus I must be very careful; the aim was to determine the circle of relations among the monitored ...'

After he left the army Plettenberg primarily worked with younger officers, who were capable of what was needed during what was known as the 'German insurrection'. One of these officers was Horst Teichgräber. This young company commander became acquainted with Plettenberg in IR 415. Before the outbreak of war he studied theology and after the war became superintendent of the Protestant Church. Teichgräber wrote to Plettenberg's son in 1995: 'It was my heartfelt desire to finally express my gratitude that your father had opened my eyes in good time to the fact that Hitler needed to be disposed of.' He recounted a conversation which he had with Plettenberg in the Dutch Palace in March 1942:

> After some introductory remarks he asked me to follow him onto the balcony where we could not be overheard. His first sentence immediately established clarity: 'We must kill Hitler!' Then he continued that he got to know me as a courageous officer in the field. The SS apparently was already withdrawing leading people from the field for a final confrontation. Therefore it was his aim to take some officers into his confidence and win them for the decisive battle for Hitler's removal.

Teichgräber raised no objections to the suggestion to kill Hitler. He followed the New Testament: 'One has to obey God more than

Man'. Yet he was worried about what would happen afterwards. 'He [Plettenberg] explained to me that we would have to negotiate a peace treaty with the Allied Forces. ... A military government would need to be installed.'

Joachim von Willisen, Plettenberg's friend and comrade from IR9, who after several wounds was working as chief inspector of forests in the Reich Forestry Office in Berlin and was later intended as political officer for the military district of Szczecin in case of a successful takeover, had similar recollections after the war:

> Plettenberg was one of the most talented and kind people I have ever met in my life. And yet he in particular was the one who in the end convinced me that there was no alternative to Hitler's elimination. For a Christian murder is one of the greatest sins, even the murder of a tyrant. Yet he also has to know that there are times during which a man has to deliberately shoulder iniquity to avert a greater wrong. All these discussions ended in the tormenting question whether the coup would still succeed in time.

The conspirators' considerations also included the possibility of suicide, if the uprising failed. Carl-Hans von Hardenberg himself notes in his *Memories of the 20th July 1944*:

> Failure, we had known for months, meant death to us all. That could not deter us, as we had to face this possibility in the time of preparation. We were willing to commit suicide in that case, although we were aware that this had to be condemned from a Christian point of view. Yet the honour of a nobleman demanded this authoritatively. The methods of medieval torture, to which the Gestapo had already subjected a large number of our friends arrested before 20th July, left open the danger that names would slip out due to physical weakness. Nobody wanted to become guilty of that kind of betrayal.

Both Hardenberg and Plettenberg later kept their word, each in his own manner. The friends also discussed that additional ethical imperatives had to be broken for the conspiracy and what this fact meant for the officers. Hardenberg continues:

> We were officers and had taken the oath of allegiance. I myself had been brought up in the strict Potsdam school which was a role model for the entire Prussian-German army. Only one who himself was borne into this mindset can conceive what it meant to take the step before us. To this was added that during the execution of the assassination as intended now also innocent people had to lose their lives. I recall an intense discussion of this point with my old friend Kurt Plettenberg who for a while was walking in silence beside me and then came to a halt and said: 'No, it's no good, even if you yourself had to die in this attempt, I would do it, the duty to the people has to be more important to us than our friendship.'

Hardenberg coined the term 'inner circle', to mean those who had supported a military coup in the past and had been aware of, or even involved in, the various failed assassination attempts. To this belonged men who way back had supported an overthrow carried out by the military and had been let in on individual – failed – assassination attempts or even had participated in them. A civilian since 1942, Plettenberg was among them, but was not involved in the planning of the military details of *Valkyrie*. Due to a lack of written sources, which for understandable reasons were few and far between, we know little about the details. We have to rely on the oral and written statements of the survivors. We learn that Plettenberg played an important role during the preparation of the assassination attempt of 20 July from a statement given in English by Carl-Hans von Hardenberg on 10 February 1947 on behalf of the *Relief Organisation 20th July 1944* in Nörten-Hardenberg in the presence of the lawyer Fabian von Schlabrendorff. Hardenberg honoured the work of his friend

Plettenberg in the resistance against Hitler with the following words: 'When the irresponsible politics of the Nazis led to war in 1939, he volunteered unconditionally for a revolutionary act. Baron von Plettenberg had a leading part in all preparations for the plot of 20 July 1944. He belonged to the intimate circle of friends of Count Stauffenberg, Minister Popitz, Colonel-General Beck and Ambassador von Hassell. All these men have like him given their lives for their convictions ...

In 1943 and 1944 he conspirators meet frequently at Neuhardenberg Castle where everything could be discussed freely in the rambling grounds. 'Each tree and each shrub reminded me of the struggle and search of the last months. ... Now the time for action had arrived. All doubts had been dispelled', Hardenberg wrote the day before the planned assassination. Amongst those who regularly visited Neuhardenberg, including Hardenberg's daughter Reinhild, named the following men:

> Claus Stauffenberg, my friend Werner Haeften, Ludwig Hammerstein, Hammerstein's father, Ewald Heinrich Kleist, Georg Sigismund Oppen, Kurt Plettenberg, Heini Lehndorff, Fritzi-Dietlof Schulenburg, the ambassador in Moscow Friedrich Werner Schulenburg, Fritz Jäger, Ulrich Hassell, Axel von dem Bussche, Friedrich Karl Klausing, the university professor Eduard Spranger, the economist Werner Sombart, Eduard von Oldenburg-Januschau, not to mention Ludwig Beck, and so on ... In the last one and half years we were as a rule visited by our 'traitor friends', as we called them, the true friends during that time.

In a later account she added Nikolaus von Halem and Fabian von Schlabrendorff.

Plettenberg's close link to Neuhardenberg during this time was also confirmed by the journalist Ursula von Kardorff. On 18 September 1943 she wrote in her diary: 'Towards evening I am with Kurt Plettenberg on the viewing platform in the forest. In

Neuhardenberg everybody fits together, as if they are cast in the same mould. For a long time we spoke about Kleist whom he loves very much as well. Plettenberg is always cheerful, I cannot not imagine at all how he would look like in a bad mood.'

Ursula von Kardorff acted as a go-between for the conspirators. In her diary the following can found: 'Fritzi [Schulenburg] asked me to deliver a letter on his behalf to Plettenberg's office in the Crown Prince's Palace.' Renate von Hardenberg, wife of Carl-Hans von Hardenberg, recounted that Plettenberg, 'who was with us very often', never wrote his name into the guest book 'because he felt like a close relative of ours'.

In her memoir *On Ever-changing Paths* Reinhild Hardenberg gives a more likely reason for Plettenberg's refusal to sign the guest book: 'As a matter of prudence some visitors like Kurt Baron von Plettenberg had avoided making an entry in the guest book in order not to expose themselves recklessly. I myself shy away from mandatory entries in guest books since 25 July [the day of her arrest].' Plettenberg indeed acted prudently, for the Gestapo confiscated the guest book after 20 July and thus gained an extensive insight into the circle of conspirators who met in this house.

Plettenberg was not only closely connected to the different members of the opposition and conspirators. Since 1942 he had also considered the possibility of killing Hitler himself. Both Marion Countess Dönhoff and Axel von dem Bussche recall that he considered shooting Hitler on 21 March 1943 during the wreath-laying ceremony at the Tomb of the Unknown Soldier. Marion Dönhoff wrote:

> As general agent of the Hohenzollern family he lived in the so-called Dutch Palace on Unter den Linden opposite the guardhouse next to the armoury. When I visited him there one day, he had just returned from big game hunting, the telescope rifle was still lying on the table. 'Look', he said, picked up the weapon without aiming it and pointed to the guardhouse [Die Neue Wache] in which the Tomb of the

Unknown Soldier was located, 'when he makes his appearance there, I could easily shoot him.'

She added: 'Yet to kill Hitler single-handedly, that would have been against his nature.' Axel von dem Bussche, however, had a different point of view:

> At what time Plettenberg considered already to use force I cannot say. But certainly he has been informed about plans of General Hoepner during the Sudeten-Crisis, which led to the Munich agreement. With this it should be said, that evolutionary thoughts alone were not sufficient. The crystallisation of such necessities in the face of rounding up and driving Jewish minorities in ghettos has been anticipated.

Axel von dem Bussche mentioned another of Plettenberg's motivations – the atrocities committed against the Jews and other minorities in the East. Both of them had witnessed this in 1940 on the Vistula. Von dem Bussche reported:

> Later, Plettenberg was already back in Berlin, I told him of the system of extermination of minorities in the Ukraine. He inquired further how many people according to our impression, we who had witnessed the first operation, had been murdered in the worst case. We had come to the conclusion that even the grimmest estimates would not add up to more than a million. He disagreed and predicted that at the end of the war as many defenceless victims murdered in the shadow of German arms would have to be lamented as fallen German soldiers on all fronts. He expected that new chemical processes would decimate the Jewish population, estimated at 20 million before the war, by at least a quarter … After this conversation Plettenberg led me to the window in his office. Diagonally opposite was the Tomb of the Unknown Soldier inside the 'guardhouse'. … Plettenberg said very calmly he could do the necessary thing during the

annual wreath-laying ceremony by the head of state. He could shoot the Führer.

Bussche adds: 'Now I do not believe that he was not man enough to do it.' Yet there were in place 'specific, quasi-programmatic blocks in the unbroken monarchist tradition … It was … taboo.' Bussche also refers to another important aspect bothering Plettenberg. What consequences would such a solo act involved, as necessary as a liberating deed of resistance would be from the inside? When would the right time be for it? 'He would ask pensively how we could ever live free again, if we did not liberate ourselves without outside help from this scourge – irrespective of political or strategic expediency. Is a single-handed attempt, if technically feasible, and notwithstanding public reaction, acceptable? Is single-handed action regardless of the consequences necessary?' Would the killing of Hitler at that time perhaps have turned the Führer into a martyr, after the victories in Poland and France, North Africa and Russia? Was the German populace ready for his overthrow? And would it have been enough to eliminate Hitler, if there was the danger that his followers would continue to rule? Such concerns were also voiced by Kurt von Hammerstein, the former head of army command and an opponent of Hitler since 1933. Even in spring 1943, on his deathbed in the Charité hospital in Berlin, he cautioned Plettenberg: 'Germany's total defeat cannot be averted by anyone. Therefore we should guard against overthrowing Hitler prematurely. First the entire populace must have realised where it had been led by this man. A new stab-in-the-back legend must not arise.' And he added: 'Kurdel, do not do it too early, the people have to go along!' Hardenberg writes about this: 'We have taken this view seriously and could not deny its validity. If we did not follow it in the end, then because of the consideration that it was the duty of those seeing clearly of not letting the German youth die pointlessly anymore and to put an end to the destruction of German towns and monuments. In contrast to that what did it matter if the few people ready to sacrifice themselves only found recognition later?'

A third aspect later mentioned by Axel von dem Bussche was the responsibility borne by Plettenberg at that time for the members of the Hohenzollern family. If the general agent of the Prussian royal house had made an attempt on the Führer's life, its representatives would have found themselves most certainly on the arrest and death lists of the Gestapo. Plettenberg was thus not only responsible for his family, himself and his friends in the resistance:

> He asked the question whether in case of failure he was allowed to become responsible for adding this comparatively small group of people to the lists of 'unworthy life' from the Polish intelligentsia ... to ethnic, religious and national minorities to militant Communists, incurably ill and cripples. Approaches of this kind were not lacking. The methods of the system did not even require written orders for this. Verbal instructions in Mafia style were sufficient.

After the war Arianne von Plettenberg wrote to the author Reinhold Schneider of the 'very grave pangs of conscience and internal battles which preoccupied my husband day and night, this obligation to become deliberately guilty in order to restore the reputation, this terrible entanglement of good and evil, from which he suffered so much, and yet he decided to act despite the belief that it was too late and but had to be done.' Marion Dönhoff observed that her friends associated with the resistance "all (became) very religious at the end, more than they had been before." The faith formed a bulwark against the impositions of the criminal reime and offered a refuge from the emotional burdens placed onto those who risked their life and the lives of their families daily through their work for the resistance.

Along these lines Plettenberg wrote in a long letter to his godson, Wilfried Berg, on the occasion of his confirmation in April 1944 that he could not agree with the widespread view 'that we humans no longer need a Christian church'. Despite 'all undeniable errors and sins of both confessions' he gives him the advice: 'it is worthwhile pondering whether the notion "For what shall it profit a man, if he shall gain the whole world, and lose his own soul?" alone is not sufficient to protect the entire Christian church from this cheap derision.' And he added in clarification that confessional formulas did not matter, 'not a more or less thoughtless "believes", but that it matters to earnestly examine to which inner attitude Christ wanted to lead the people in their relationship to each other, in their relation to death and God, as both are closely linked.' Plettenberg was probably also speaking to himself here, when he made a profession of undogmatically following Christ and of a faith in God not fearing death. This 'inner attitude' profoundly influenced his activity in the resistance. He remained faithful to it in the difficult months that followed.

Meanwhile the preparations for Operation *Valkyrie* continued. After the bombing of the Dutch Palace in November 1943 and his relocation to Cecilienhof Castle in Potsdam, Kurt von Plettenberg immediately resumed his role as advisor to the resistance. Due to his extensive military and civilian contacts he is able to provide the various groups of resistance with his knowledge, in particular of people.

Eberhard Zeller, who was the first historian after the war to interview the few survivors of the 20 July 1944 plot, wrote:

> In Stauffenberg's inner group his cousin Count von Yorck ...,
> Adam von Trott zu Solz ..., Hans Bernd von Haeften ..., Carl-
> Hans Count von Hardenberg ..., Kurt Baron von Plettenberg,
> general agent (and president of the chamber) of the former
> Prussian royal house, open to a new political thinking, valued as
> much for his unassuming nobility as for his reliability, have to be
> named as advisors and political allies ready to take on tasks ...

Zeller wrote to Plettenberg's son that 'decades later I heard Axel von dem Bussche, Margarete von Oven [Tresckow's and Stauffenberg's secretary] and Marion Countess Dönhoff speaking of him with great admiration.'

When Count Lehndorff wanted to check the reliability of Axel von dem Bussche, who in autumn 1943 declared himself willing to blow up Hitler during a presentation of new winter uniforms, Plettenberg vouched for his trustworthiness.

Within the resistance network, Dönhoff, Bussche, Lehndorff, Plettenberg, Tresckow, Heinrich Count zu Dohna who was in contact with Marion Dönhoff, and also Groeben formed a special axis of trust. This team spirit had developed in East Prussia.

In Potsdam, still untouched by the bombing raids, the different resistance groups meet in various apartments to exchange information, to recruit kindred spirits and to flesh out their plans. Venues included the houses of Ferdinand von Lüninck, the former governor of the Rhine province, or of Gottfried von Bismarck-Schönhausen, District President of Potsdam, where Plettenberg, Adam von Trott zu Solz, Ulrich von Hassell, the Berlin police president Count Wolf-Heinrich Helldorf, and further people privy to the plot in varying degrees met. A series of such meetings in Berlin, in which Plettenberg participated, are reported to have taken place at the Esplanade hotel and the apartment of Ola Rüdt von Collenberg by Karl Ludwig von Guttenberg, Joachim von Willisen and Fritz-Dietlof von der Schulenburg. Mady von Schilling later reported that she and her sister Birgit (nieces of Carl-Hans von Hardenberg) often held parties for friends on Saturdays which served as cover for meetings of the inner group. The conspirators locked themselves into the air-raid shelters for that purpose.

At the beginning of 1944 Caesar von Hofacker's confidant Gotthard von Falkenhausen travelled as his emissary from the Western Front in Paris to Berlin:

> At the request of Hofacker in January and February 1944 I went to Berlin for two days respectively and in Stauffenberg's apartment in Nikolassee made contact with his uncle and confidant Count Üxküll, and further spoke at length with my friend von Plettenberg in Potsdam. We established that the matters would be driven forward on the lines discussed, however without being able to fix a means or date for the first strike. Every assassination remains a spontaneous act to a

certain degree, born from a sudden opportunity; it cannot be artificially planned like a military operation and on the basis of theoretical considerations. Primarily it is important to find the person suitable for this first strike, who was above suspicion and at the same time had access and the right to report at the highest level. Both Üxküll and Plettenberg expressed themselves despondently about the uncomprehending and fainthearted attitude of the high-ranking generals who despite knowing better could not find it in themselves to decide on responsible action.

They also discussed the potential response abroad to such an act, and they had few illusions about the attitude of the British government which so far had not reacted positively to any of the attempts to make contact through emissaries by Goerdeler or Canaris. Therefore there was the danger that every new government after an overthrow would be empty-handed and a new stab-in-the-back legend had to be anticipated.

Regardless of this, Adam von Trott zu Solz and Hans Bernd Gisevius still made an offer to negotiate on behalf of Goerdeler in the spring of 1944 in Geneva. Through contacts to the head of the US secret service, Allen W. Dulles, they wanted to avoid Germany's unconditional surrender, as it had been decided in 1942 during the Casablanca conference by the Western Powers. The reactions were not unambiguous and contributed to the fact that illusions about possible political room for manoeuvre persisted among the conspirators.

Stauffenberg also still believed in such a solution and sent a representative to Madrid to make contact with Eisenhower. They hoped to exploit mutual hostility to the Bolshevist enemy in the East. The landing of the Allied forces in Normandy in June 1944, however, finally brought home to the conspirators that the *coup d'état* had come too late for any expectations of this kind and that any hopes of a negotiated peace were gone. Henning von Tresckow drew the following conclusion: 'The assassination has to be carried out at all costs. If it fails, we have to act in Berlin nonetheless. For the practical purpose no longer matters, but that the German resistance movement has dared the decisive deed in the face of the world and history. Everything else is irrelevant besides this.' Tresckow's confidant, Heinrich von Lehndorff, conveyed these words to Stauffenberg who as a consequence decided to carry out the assassination himself. Fritz-Dietlof von der Schulenburg had similar thoughts, as recorded by Kunrat von Hammerstein: 'Apparently the German people have to drain this cup to the dregs. We have to sacrifice ourselves, we will be understood later ... Yes, a gesture, yet a very important gesture. To have cleansed ourselves from within is most important for us and our place in the world, even at the last moment.'

Stauffenberg made three attempts to carry out the assassination during July 1944. On 6 and 11 July he had the explosives with him at the briefing at the Berghof in Berchtesgaden, and then on 15 July at the Führer headquarters which had been relocated to the 'Wolf's Lair' in East Prussia. Each time Stauffenberg hesitated because Göring and Himmler, whose simultaneous removal was considered essential by all involved, were not present. The last, decisive, meeting took place in Stauffenberg's Berlin apartment on 16 July. The assassination had to be carried out during the next conference scheduled for 20 July at the 'Wolf's Lair' whatever the situation. The results are known.

Shortly before 20 July Plettenberg left for Bückeburg. It has to be assumed that as a civilian he had no specific tasks to perform in the seizure of power in Berlin, and also that his concern for the former Prussian royal house mentioned above played a part in this decision. He must have feared the Gestapo would drag the Hohenzollerns into the plot if their general agent was exposed as part of the conspiracy.

Therefore, on his return to Berlin on 24 July he could only stand by helplessly when he learnt that most of his co-conspirators had either been shot or arrested, among them his friend Carl-Hans Hardenberg. He learnt that Henning von Tresckow was dead and that the Gestapo had also arrested the wives and daughters of his friends.

Chapter 11

After the Failure of Operation *Valkyrie*

After the failed attempt to seize power on 20 July 1944 Claus Schenk von Stauffenberg, Albrecht Mertz von Quirnheim, Friedrich Olbricht and Werner von Haeften were court-martialled and shot at the Bendlerblock in Berlin. Ludwig Beck's attempt at suicide failed but he subsequently received a coup de grace. On the same night a wave of arrests commenced encompassing more than 600 persons.

Henning von Tresckow, Hans-Ulrich von Oertzen, Eduard Wagner and Wessel von Freytag-Loringhoven killed themselves in the days immediately following 20 July. Suicide attempts by Carl-Heinrich von Stülpnagel and Carl-Hans von Hardenberg failed. Stülpnagel was hauled before the People's Court and executed on 20 August. The Gestapo imprisoned the seriously injured Hardenberg in the Oranienburg-Sachsenhausen concentration camp near Berlin. Hans-Alexander von Voß committed suicide on 8 November 1944 to avoid arrest.

Among the arrested were many well-known people such as the former Reich Ministers Hjalmar Schacht and Gustav Noske as well as the Prussian Minister of Finance Johannes Popitz who were part of the conspiracy. The retired General Franz Halder and the former ambassador Ulrich von Hassell, the head of counterintelligence Wilhelm Canaris and his deputy Hans Oster shared their fate. Carl Goerdeler was caught on 12 August during his flight to East Prussia.

Four young officers who had been ready to make assassination attempts – Axel von dem Bussche, Rudolph-Christoph von Gersdorff, Ewald-Heinrich von Kleist-Schmenzin and Eberhard von Breitenbuch – were never discovered by the Gestapo. The prisoners never gave up their names during interrogation despite 'intensified examination', as torture methods were referred to.

Following the first wave of arrests, Operation 'Thunderstorm' on 17 August saw the rounding-up of roughly 5,000 members of parliament and officials of the old parties, among them Konrad Adenauer and Kurt Schumacher, who for the most part vanished into concentration camps for weeks or months, some remaining there until the end of the war. Thus it was hoped to nip any further opposition in the bud. Hitler's revenge was also directed against the families of the conspirators, among them numerous wives and children who, on the order of Ernst Kaltenbrunner, head of the Reich Security Main Office, were arrested on the grounds of 'familial responsibility'.

As early as the beginning of August 1944 trials before the People's Court began. Chaired by Roland Freisler, the court imposed the death penalty in the majority of cases. If Hitler considered a sentence too lenient, he revoked it and had it increased by another court. Those admitted to or ordered to attend the proceedings were sworn to secrecy, but nevertheless details got out. Ursula von Kardorff, for example, regularly heard of Freisler's sadistic conduct and the often admirable composure of the accused from her colleagues on the *Deutsche Allgemeine Zeitung* who had to attend the proceedings. She noted in her diary on 8 September 1944: 'Count Douglas and Döring had already returned at lunchtime from the proceedings. They came back like ghosts. They were still so upset that everything simply spilled out from them, although they had sworn secrecy. Freisler in his scarlet robes screamed from 9am to noon …'

Also the statements the accused made in court despite Freisler's attempts to shout them down became known. Fritz-Dietlof von Schulenburg stated frankly: 'We have shouldered this deed to preserve Germany from unnamed misery. I am aware that as a consequence I will be hanged, but do not regret my deed and hope that another will execute it at a more fortunate time. Field Marshal General von Witzleben confronted Freisler as follows: 'You can deliver us to the executioner. Three months from now the tortured people will rise up and bring you to justice and drag you alive through the dirt of the streets.' Hans-Bernd von Haeften dared to say: 'According to the opinion which I have of the Führer's role in world history, he is a great force for evil . . .', He could not go on, as Freisler shouted him down, but he had wanted to say that he, therefore, did not feel himself bound by any oath to the Führer.

Conspirators were still being executed right up until the end of the war, most by hanging. However, Freisler himself was killed during a bombing raid on 3 February 1945 while crossing the patio of the People's Court. He was still holding the files of the proceedings against Fabian von Schlabrendorff. Schlabrendorff was at first acquitted after the loss of the files, but immediately rearrested by the Gestapo, brought to Prinz-Albrecht-Straße and subsequently sent to Flossenbürg, where he was finally liberated by the Americans shortly before the end of the war together with a number of other prisoners who had been imprisoned on the basis of collective responsibility. In total at least 180 people were executed or committed suicide as a result of the failed assassination.

* * *

Plettenberg and Hardenberg had agreed to commit suicide in case of arrest to ensure that they would not betray any fellow conspirators under interrogation by the Gestapo. When Hardenberg was arrested in Neuhardenberg three days after the attempted *coup d'état*, he shot himself in the chest and then slit his wrists. But he survived and was sent to Oranienburg-Sachsenhausen. With the aid of Communist fellow prisoners and a French doctor who wrote him sick notes, he managed to survive in the camp hospital block until the liberation.

Hardenberg was in the Bendlerblock on 20 July, although he was at first intended for a civilian task after the overthrow. He later writes that he wanted 'to be with his friends during this fateful hour'. However, he was not arrested because of this, as he was able to cover up that he had been there for a short time, but because he was on the lists of conspirators which fell into the hands of the Gestapo. He was supposed to become governor of Berlin and Mark Brandenburg. In addition the Neuhardenberg guest book was seized in which the names Stauffenberg, Haeften, Beck, Hammerstein and others were noted. This incriminated him further in the Gestapo's eyes. Renate von Hardenberg wrote:

> Unfortunately our guest book was very revealing and many people have been questioned about us in hours of examinations. Yet if we had disposed of it, it would have been even more dangerous, as they would have then questioned the staff regarding our associations and would have involved even more people. ... It was telling for our friends' attitude that they did not hesitate to write their names into the guest book and thus confirm the connection. They supposed that – if the overthrow failed – all would be lost anyway. Only Plettenberg who stayed with us very frequently never wrote down his name ...

In contrast, Plettenberg was not mentioned on any of the conspirators' lists for jobs during or after the takeover, although he was involved in the preparations for it. Therefore, he remained undetected at first.

Axel von dem Bussche explained that Plettenberg saw himself confronted with a very personal dilemma as general agent of the former ruling house and president of the court chamber of the house of Schaumburg-Lippe. The mood in radical Nazi circles was hostile to the nobility. Sensationalist articles in *Der Stürmer* agitated against the 'aristocracy infested by Jews'. Friedrich Hielscher, who knew how the Nazis thought, told Axel von dem

Bussche and Fritz-Dietlof von der Schulenburg that 'they were only waiting for the right moment to include the members of the pre-1918 ruling houses among the other minorities to be eradicated and to "confiscate" their assets'. Bussche added: 'This was the reason for not including Plettenberg's name in the fateful list.'

Plettenberg's family tradition of loyalty to the Hohenzollerns remained firm, but there was no such tie to Hitler, despite the soldier's oath. The Führer had no place in the Prussian tradition. The men planning 'high treason' had already identified Hitler as a force for evil, as Hans-Bernd von Haeftern had said to Freisler, and this had released them from their oath. Plettenberg therefore felt no scruples about killing Hitler himself, but had to consider the possible consequences of his actions for the former Prussian royal house. He felt obliged to protect its members.

The arrest and murder of his friends and fellow conspirators by the Gestapo during the weeks and months after the failed takeover shocked Plettenberg deeply. His father-in-law Helmuth von Maltzahn was also arrested on 21 July 1944. He had made no secret of his rejection of the Nazis and was, therefore, suspected of being part of the conspiracy. He was held in the local prison in Greifswald, but was released after three months as nothing could be proved against him.

In the weeks and months after the failed assassination all that Plettenberg could do was try to help those who had been arrested as much as he could. He was particularly concerned with the fate of his friend Hardenberg. Renate von Hardenberg wrote:

> Later I met him [Plettenberg] occasionally, when I was at his house in Unter den Linden 11 to see the lawyer Kurt Sievert [who was representing the seriously-ill prisoner Hardenberg]. Kurdel had the most audacious plans to liberate Hanni, but we agreed that by that alone nothing would be gained. Where for instance should he stay? In his state he could not be hidden like the Hammersteins. He

would be too easily recognisable. We also discussed approaching Himmler, which perhaps was not so far-fetched. But by no means did I want to write a 'plea for mercy'.

In a letter to his wife dated 20 August 1944, Plettenberg was deeply worried about his friend's health. He refers to the tall Hardenberg in his letter as 'the little fellow' to conceal his identity. After all the latter had been through, he did not consider him very resilient. Yet he could not see any way to help his friend. He had to remain passive. He wanted to be at the front now. He could not help himself, as he once wrote to his cousin:

> On the other hand I am not so devoid of self-awareness that I did not know how irrelevant it is in the grand scheme of things if an elderly major no longer familiar with every matter of warfare takes part somewhere or not. It may be the case that the most difficult and greatest tasks for the living are still ahead of us.

A letter to Marion Dönhoff showed that as early as mid-June 1944 he had requested his reinstatement as an officer at the Eastern Front: 'But will they turn to an officer out of action for two and a half years with the still existing surplus of experienced candidates? It is wholly against my nature to sit at home while the battle for East Prussia is raging.' As he was not intended for an active role in the pending coup, he wanted to fight at the front rather than spend the time waiting. The reference to East Prussia showed the close connection he felt to his second home after the years at Friedrichstein, which furthermore evokes the figure of his ancestor Wolter von Plettenberg. The advance of the Red Army in East Prussia must have moved him profoundly.

Perhaps the decision to apply for active service again was influenced by the desire to rid himself of the burdens and constraints bearing down on him. Not by coincidence he marked a passage on the effect of war on the individual in René Quinton's book *The Voice of War*:

All fetters of society have fallen away: the torment of the career, the worry about the professional conduct, the difference in class, the injustice of promotion, the loneliness, the wearing down and the doubt of standing in the right place, goals which cannot be achieved by any courage or exertion, the entire network of temptations, the frictions of life and the mediocrity of the whole situation. The entire life of society is artificial: the war shatters it. It is the benefit of war that he returns man to the original life.

On 11 August Kurt von Plettenberg inquired once again of the assistant general headquarters 'whether despite my age – I am 54 years old – service at the front is still possible for me.' On 26 August 1944 he receives a negative reply to his application for redeployment from the headquarters of III Army Corps. The reason given to him by a Colonel Wiese is that 'fairly high requirements are still demanded' from the commanders of battalions and regiments 'which you probably no longer meet despite your known freshness and flexibility'. Whether he likes it or not Plettenberg submits to this decision, though he replies to the colonel: 'On the other hand I can claim for myself without boasting that I have had a steady hand with my soldiers and that I have never experienced any deep disappointment with my troops even in the most difficult times … I thus have to see how matters will proceed and if I might be useful at home. '

He became more and more despondent. He had escaped the first wave of arrests unscathed, but what can the future still mean for him without his familiar friends and with the continuing destruction of everything he felt was worth living for? In a letter dated March 1945 his sister-in-law Veronika von Maltzahn recalled:

I remember very clearly – during my last get-together with Kurt in spring here at Schossow we spoke about it – that Kurt was very familiar with the notion of death and almost longed for it and only found still joy in life because of Nanni whom he found it difficult to leave behind. Yet he nevertheless filled this life with feverish work, the desire to help and a deep joy in his domestic happiness which was truly and infinitely valuable and necessary for his inner balance. Apart from that the difference between death and life seemed marginally to him and he never found there to be a deep rift between them.

Full of foreboding, he had already written to Marion Dönhoff in May 1944: 'Who knows which tasks life will bring us? And if there is a different outcome and we have no future, then we want to be grateful for what we had and try to live in a way that the end will be a dignified one.'

Despite this depressive mood, Plettenberg does not seem to have given up completely. Efforts to remove Hitler did not come to an end after 20 July 1944. How much knowledge Kurt von Plettenberg had of new plans to overthrow Hitler, or how far he was even involved in them, has not been completely resolved.

Axel von dem Bussche gave an indication. He recalled his last evening with Plettenberg in Potsdam, shortly before the end of 1944:

And then came Plettenberg's report of an unannounced surprise visit by Albert Speer in autumn 1944. Speer implored him, Plettenberg, to activate any existing contacts to the English, for now the Führer had to be removed. Reporting this, Plettenberg said he only listened, saying nothing, as it seemed possible to him that Speer, whom he only knew in passing, wanted to get him to betray himself. Speer then left him alone and did not appear again. Now, after thorough consideration, he, Plettenberg, considered it possible that Speer – in his way honestly and seriously worried – had come with a real proposition, even if emotional and amateurishly careless. Plettenberg blamed himself for having missed possibly the last opportunity to put a stop to further crimes and destruction ... Through no fault of his own, Kurt von

Plettenberg had been sucked helplessly into a whirlpool of emotions which had driven him, usually so calm, into an abyss of despair.

However, in his memoirs published in 1969, Speer wrote that he personally decided to remove Hitler only at the beginning of February 1945, when he planned a gas attack on Hitler's bunker which had to be abandoned when in March he found that SS guards had been posted on the roof of the complex in question. Since the veracity of much of Speer's memoirs is rightly in doubt today, this account should be regarded with reservation.

August Winnig, the former governor of East Prussia, who met Plettenberg on a few occasions after 20 July at Cecilienhof and in his own house, would later state that Plettenberg had been informed of new plans for an overthrow, but also that shortly before his arrest he was deeply pessimistic, not only regarding their chances of success but also in general. Winnig, who was not privy to the details of the 20 July plot, recalled:

> [Plettenberg had] hoped until late into autumn … for an insurgency by large parts of the Wehrmacht. He was close to the military groups and knew more than he said. It was already the middle of January 1945 when he invited me through a member of the castle staff. We were sitting in his room. …'I wish to tell you what I think', he began. 'All our actions were attempts to escape destiny. We felt or we knew where things were heading and struggled against it. Hoepner was the first to attempt it; I do not know how far his connections reached, but the first strike would have certainly succeeded and with it he would have created a new situation; Hitler's removal would have prevented the war. Then the most unlikely thing happens and Hitler returns from Munich as a preserver of peace and Hoepner withdraws. In summer 1942 a pilot officer goes stalking near the Führer's headquarters. Permission to do so was rarely granted, but he

had received it. He hears something, takes cover and cocks the rifle. On the path Hitler appears, on his own without any escort. The pilot sees him and thinks: this is the decisive hour, now he shall die. He wants to aim, but he cannot lift the rifle, his arms give out. He secures the rifle and hangs it over his shoulder – that he is able to do – and walks on. Hitler turns pale when he sees him. The pilot salutes, and Hitler, looking alarmed, returns the greeting and passes by. In 1943 we were ready twice – each time we had to stop. Last summer the plan had to be postponed twice more. When finally everything seems to fit, and everything is ready, he remains unharmed.

Now in autumn [1944] once more the opportunity for a large-scale action rose and it dissolved into nothing. All this was a battle against fate. The 20th July was a last rebellion against doom, hence against something which is imposed on us. We are standing at the abyss – there is no salvation. God's will is stronger than our resistance.

In the last weeks before his arrest Kurt von Plettenberg was primarily concerned with the preservation of the Hohenzollern estate. In the winter of 1944/45, the issue was to store valuables of great historic value in places which offered safety according to the assessment at that time. The Hohenzollern museum at Monbijou Castle in Berlin had been unsafe since 1943 due to the constant bombing. The collections were evacuated to Weimar, Oels and Cecilienhof castle in Potsdam, but most of these precious items were lost in the chaos of war.

Plettenberg's gave special attention to the Prussian royal crown which Wilhelm II had redesigned in 1889 after the model of the previous crown, and fifteen golden snuffboxes which once belonged to Frederick the Great. In August 1943, due to the bombing they were taken by the Chief of Cabinet von Müldner from the Crown strongroom in Berlin and brought in two tin boxes soldered shut to Cecilienhof castle in Potsdam where they were bricked in in a safe for the time being. In a short note dated 8 February 1945 found after the war Plettenberg recorded that he 'transferred the two boxes in the night of 6th February [1945] to Bückeburg and bricked them in at a safe place'.

After initial enquiries, around Christmas he made contact with Martin Strathmann, a former officer with the Bückeburger Jäger and now a clergyman in Kleinenbremen near Bückeburg. Saying 'Prussia looks for old Prussians', von Plettenberg allegedly asked the old clergyman for help and he immediately agreed to hide the valuables in his church.

In Bückeburg Plettenberg stuffed both boxes into a backpack and at night hiked 4km across snow-covered fields to Kleinenbremen. There Strathmann, the sexton Friedrich Aldag and an old master bricklayer, Wilhelm Ackermann, were waiting for him. They descended the stairway to a crypt below the choir of the neo-Gothic church. In a niche under the stars they store the two boxes. Ackermann built a wall, plastered it and rubbed coal dust into the grout to erase their traces.

Only a few knew of the treasure in the church. Those involved all remained silent. Yet after the end of war the British found the aforementioned note in the files of the court chamber office of Schaumburg-Lippe, as well as a sketch by Plettenberg with hints to the contents of the boxes.

On 3 January the British occupying troops summon Prince Oskar of Prussia, the representative of the Crown Prince being detained in Hechingen, to Bückeburg. In order not to reveal the hiding place, he demanded that the British royal house related to the Hohenzollerns had to be involved. Yet the commission of the occupying force refused this. It threatened to confiscate the objects as *bona vacantia*. Prince Oskar gave in. In the protocol signed by him it states:

'In February 1945 valuables of the Crown Prince were evacuated in agreement with Mr von Plettenberg and Mr von Müldner, namely to the region around of Bückeburg. This fact was known to me, likewise the intended place, but not the contents of the consignment. Mr von Plettenberg then arranged and carried out everything else here. He had bricked in the objects in the church of Kleinenbremen.'

The next day, in Kleinenbremen, the hiding place was opened in the presence of the surprised minister Strathmann. The boxes were taken into safe keeping, being placed in the safe of the Reichsbank branch in Minden. After a long legal dispute it was acknowledged that they were the private property of the Hohenzollerns private estate and did not belong to the state. Two and a half years after the discovery, on 17 September 1948, Carl-Hans Count von Hardenberg, Plettenberg's friend and successor as general agent of the former Prussian royal house, took delivery of the treasure once more, with the exception of one snuffbox. Today the royal crown and some of the snuffboxes can be seen again at Hechingen Castle, ancestral seat of the Hohenzollerns. Seven snuffboxes are on long-term loan to Charlottenburg Castle in Berlin. Their former hiding place in the church of Kleinenbremen can also be visited.

In the last weeks of February 1945 Plettenberg was initially in Bückeburg. Here the war had left its mark. Arianne von Plettenberg not only had her own three little children to look after in spring 1945. In addition, her mother and her youngest sister Hadumoth, who had fled Western Pomerania from the Red Army together with her Dutch sister-in-law Anna-Mathilde von Maltzahn, the latter's two-month-old twin sons and a nurse, and also Elsa von Maltzahn, her half-Jewish aunt who had already sought shelter with her after fleeing Berlin in 1943, had to be cared for. Including the servants, twelve people were now in the house. Yvonne von Kuenheim, Marion Dönhoff's older sister, and her sister-in-law Sissi neé Lehndorff with her three children, on Plettenberg's advice, had first found shelter with his family in Bückeburg at first and then in the neighbouring Bad Eilsen with the ophthalmologist Friedrich von Tippelskirch.

According to his wife and the Dönhoffs, Plettenberg was suffering great inner turmoil during these weeks, since he believed that he still needed to manage the affairs of the Hohenzollerns in Potsdam. His family and friends tried in vain to dissuade him from his intended trip to Berlin and Potsdam. At first he travelled straight across the ruined country to Vorarlberg to the Crown Prince and immediately afterwards to Kissingen to Prince Louis Ferdinand to discuss the necessary measures.

On 2 March he returned to Potsdam. The day before officers of the Gestapo had asked for him. No-one could warn him, however, because he had been travelling for days on the half-destroyed railway network.

Chapter 12

Denunciation

By the end of February 1945 Plettenberg seemed to have escaped detection. He was on guard, however, and never met Renate von Hardenberg in Neuhardenberg, but only in neutral locations. He was extremely cautious, for as Tisa von der Schulenburg wrote regarding those times 'even in the closest human relationships mistrust could lie in wait: who will betray me? Who is a Nazi? Who a member of the opposition? Who is decent, even as a Nazi? And who of those, though a member of the opposition, will give in and denounce me? Who could be relied upon?'

Kurt von Plettenberg could be relied upon. Yet no reliance – Plettenberg's friends were certain of this after his arrest – could be placed upon Lieutenant Rupprecht Gehring. They suspected him of being the one who caused Plettenberg's arrest by careless boasting. Although he had to be aware of the intensive telephone surveillance, he called the Hardenbergs without any precautions. Renate von Hardenberg remembers;

> Once a First Lieutenant Gericke [sic] called who seemed to be a rather loose-tongued braggart. He said he had the opportunity to be at Führer headquarters from time to time and could exert influence there regarding the arrests. ... This man then later betrayed, perhaps only due to foolish garrulity, our dear Kurdel Plettenberg.

Von Müldner of the Hohenzollern general administration in Berlin also believed that Plettenberg had been betrayed. After his arrest he told the Reich Minister of Finance Schwerin von Krosigk on 9 March the 'impression' and the 'conviction' at Cecilienhof castle was 'that at the forefront of the Plettenberg case is the matter with the very unpleasant First Lieutenant Gehring … In any case Plettenberg looked after this man more than he deserved it and in return Gehring blabbed political things about Plettenberg, perhaps also about the House [the Hohenzollern family]'.

Schlabrendorff learnt in prison of Plettenberg's suspicion that he was betrayed by an informer. He told Plettenberg's widow in January 1946 of one of his night-time discussions with Plettenberg in the prison air-raid shelter: 'While your husband was in good spirits at the beginning, one day he resigned himself to his fate. He explained this saying he had been informed upon. From then on your husband no longer worried about himself, but his fellow conspirators. He feared he could be forced under torture to divulge names.'

Plettenberg did not assume that Gehring was this informer. Yet he suspected, as shown in another of Schlabrendorff's statements, that Gehring had triggered his arrest. Gehring and Plettenberg first came into contact through Kunrat von Hammerstein, who had known Gehring since 1941 from the staff of Guderian (a cousin of Gehring). In his memoirs Hammerstein recounted that he met Gehring, formerly a staunch Nazi who had already lost a leg during the war in 1939 and had injured his spine in Africa, again shortly before Christmas 1942, and found him now to be a decided opponent of Hitler.

> He said to someone that he wanted to kill Hitler with explosives hidden in his false leg, but I did not hear this at the time. I wrote in a letter: 'He is full of energy and wants to volunteer with the one who masters the situation from a military aspect.' … Gehring then commanded a tank company in Wünsdorf near Berlin and wanted to lead it against the government: 'I will do the reconnaissance for you.'

At the end of May 1943 Hammerstein visited Gehring, who desperately wanted to speak to Ludwig Beck, in the Charité hospital. Because this seemed too dangerous to Hammerstein, he did not make contact with Beck. Yet during this meeting he advised Gehring to visit Kurt Plettenberg at the Dutch Palace. In his memoirs Hammerstein wrote:

> Mr von Plettenberg let Gehring live in Prince Friedrich's room, for Gehring was studying agriculture after his hospital stay [due to his serious injuries he was exempt from military duties from mid-1943 onwards]. He drank tea at Cecilienhof, probably resided for a while with Count Helldorf (police president) and did his internship in summer 1944 on the estate of the emperor's second wife Hermine, where he missed the 20th July. In autumn 1944 he dragged a suitcase with machine guns across Berlin and wanted to liberate an injured conspirator guarded by the SS from the hospital (probably Count Hardenberg). Allegedly he had something big planned for the 11th, then the 16th January [1945] with some officers. On the 18th or 19th January he was arrested in Berlin by *SS-Obersturmbannführer* Valentin of the Reich Security Main Office. My brother Franz met him in the prison at Lehrter Straße. ... Gehring said that he had been on the verge of flying to England to open negotiations in the context of a new *coup d'état*.

Regarding 'the big thing with the officers ' in January 1945 mentioned by Gehring, his brother Helmut later recalled that the former confided to his mother and sister during his last visit to the Bahrendorf vicarage near Magdeburg that 'a thing had been planned for 11th January 1945 which had to be postponed, however'.

The Berlin military historian Klaus Mayer, who has for many years pursued the slightest hints of action against Hitler after 20 July 1944 and who has focussed in particular on Rupprecht Gehring, has come to the conclusion that 'the thing' might have been an intended attack on Hitler on the occasion of his return to Berlin. On 15 January 1945 Hitler left his 'Eagle's Nest' headquarters at Ziegenberg near Bad Nauheim and arrived in Berlin-Grunewald aboard his special train *Brandenburg* the next morning. During one of the customary intermediate stops, the opportunity for an attack with explosives might have presented itself. Furthermore Mayer surmises that Gehring also intended to make contact with the Western Allies. He wanted to give military support to Allied paratroop landings in the Potsdam and Berlin areas, before the Soviets arrived.

It is known that Fritz Kolbe, an official in the Foreign Office and member of the resistance, reported during his regular meetings with the head of the American OSS Allen Dulles in Geneva of plans by a Berlin resistance group numbering between 30 and 100 men who would guide American paratroopers who were supposed to land in the area of Wannsee and Schlachtensee to their targets in the city. The capital of the Reich was supposed to be taken by surprise attack before the Soviets could seize it, but perhaps the plan was only to capture Hitler in the Reich Chancellery bunker. The Americans declined, because meanwhile it had been agreed between Stalin and the Western Allies that the Soviets should take Berlin. Kunrat's brother, the theologist Franz von Hammerstein, supported his brother's story in his sworn statement of 3 April 1946:

> During some walks Gehring told me briefly that in the context of a new overthrow attempt to which for example also Mr von Plettenberg fell victim he [Gehring] had had the mission to fly to England, but had been denounced, and now was very strained. The preparations for such a flight had been too difficult. ... He was arrested because of a conversation he had with someone who probably betrayed him.

The search for the one who might have betrayed Plettenberg leads next to the then First Lieutenant and later author Bernhard Horstmann. In 1997 Horstmann published a book entitled *Prinz-*

Albrecht-Straße 8: The Authentic Account of the Last Survivor of 1945, claimed to be based on notes made in 1946–7. According to Horstmann's account the following scene took place after Gehring's transfer from the prison in Lehrter Straße to Prinz-Albrecht-Straße in March 1945:

> He [Gehring] came towards me below the basement entrance, when he was led to the latrine and I was returning from it. We were alarmed when we faced each other so unexpectedly. As the guards had remained a little behind, we had the opportunity to whisper a few words to each other. Gerhing seemed to suspect that I had reported to the police. 'You wretch', he whispered to me. I was dumbfounded. If that was the case I hardly would be here. 'W-o-l-f', I whispered back. 'How could you have done something like that, man?' He stared at me aghast, until he was dragged away by the guard. In the door he turned his horrified face to me once more. He did not seem to have had this suspicion at all.

This ominous 'Wolf' put forward by Horstmann as Gehring's informer was, according to his version, a Gestapo agent: 'Of course "Wolf" was an agent provocateur set by Office IV of the Reich Security Main Office against the Hohenzollern circle …' On 13 January 1945 Gehring allegedly took him, Horstmann, along to a meeting with 'Wolf' in the latter's apartment in Knesebeckstraße 39, Berlin. Both men, Wolf and Gehring had claimed 'to have known each other for a long time'. Yet nothing more has ever been discovered about an agent 'Wolf' in Office IV. Did Horstmann invent him to deflect blame from himself?

Furthermore, Horstmann's memoirs contain a number of inconsistencies and dubious accounts for the period of September 1944 until 28 April 1945. We can gather from the sources available that he was born in Munich in 1919 and joined the NSDAP while still at school in 1937. He volunteered at the beginning of the war as an officer candidate with the Luftwaffe (anti-aircraft artillery). In 1942 he was promoted to second lieutenant and in June 1944 to first lieutenant. In September 1944 he was on the staff of the 9th Motorised Anti-Aircraft Division. After that, he wrote that he caught a knee infection which was initially treated at a field hospital in Vienna and then went on sick leave, with his left leg in a cast, staying with his mother in Bergneustadt. During a visit to Gummersbach with a doctor friend he fell and cut his arm open, severing the artery. After an emergency operation he was questioned by the Gestapo on suspicion of deliberate self-mutilation but the surgeon who had operated on him exonerated him.

At the end of November 1944 he was sent to his regiment's replacement unit at Stralsund. As he was not needed there, at his own request he was transferred as unfit for active service to a reserve field hospital in Berlin-Spandau. In Berlin he lived away from the hospital with his half-brother Ludwig, a senior leader of the National Socialist Motor Corps and a party member since 1929.

Around Christmas 1944 he met opponents of the Nazis at the house of Mrs von Kalckreuth and there spoke for the first time with Rupprecht Gehring. Horstmann writes: 'Gehring then disclosed to me that new operations were being prepared which in his opinion would be successful.' It was the plan to land German paratroopers at the Wolf's Lair and eliminate Hitler. For this reason he had to fly to England. He, Horstmann, did not want to get involved in these plans, because they did not seem feasible to him, but he was willing to join in more carefully-planned operations. Afterwards he met several times with Gehring and the aforementioned 'Wolf' at Knesebeckstraße 39 in Berlin-Charlottenburg where he again refused to participate in the planned operation.

Shortly after this meeting he tried to get transferred back to his replacement unit in Stralsund. In fact, as can be gathered from his account, Horstmann had not needed to be in hospital for quite some time. But on 16 January 1945 he was arrested at his half-brother's house by the Gestapo and brought to the prison in Prinz-Albrecht-Straße. During his first interrogation by

Obersturmbannführer Valentin, who also questioned Gehring and later Plettenberg, as is clear from his own account, he incriminated Gehring and exonerated himself by saying that he would have made a report if he had not been arrested. At that time he thought that the Gestapo knew everything already from 'Wolf'. The name 'Wolf', however, did not trigger any reaction from his interrogator.

The contradictions continue. On 20/21 April 1945 the Red Army's assault on Berlin began. While Rupprecht Gehring, together with seventeen other prisoners, was shot by the SS during the night of 22 April, Horstmann writes that he was released on the 25th; all his possessions, including his loaded pistol, were returned to him. Afterwards he was even driven from Prinz-Albrecht-Straße to Hardenbergstraße where he claims that he joined a unit in western Berlin and was captured by the Russians on 2 May. He was released by them in October 1946.

According to the account of the Communist 'trusty' Heinz Hentschke, who had been detained in Prinz-Albrecht-Straße since April 1943, the trusties had to leave the almost completely destroyed main prison on 29 April together with the remaining SS men to participate in the final battle for the Reich Chancellery. The few remaining prisoners were left behind in the locked cells. They were liberated by the Russians on 2 May 1945, as one of them, the clergyman August Reinicke, reported. This means that Bernhard Horstmann was the only prisoner who got out of the Gestapo's main prison unscathed in the last days of the war. He explains this as being due to luck and sympathy between him and *Obersturmbannführer* Valentin.

It is surprising that nowhere in his memoirs does Horstmann mention Plettenberg or the circumstances of his death, which were certainly known by the prisoners. Plettenberg's name does not appear in the list he drew up of prisoners held at Prinz-Albrecht-Straße between 16 January and 24 April 1945, although all the other prominent members of the resistance and even the 'trusties' are in it. Horstmann claims that he only found out after the war from Gehring's brother, Ludwig, that Rupprecht had been working on a Hohenzollern estate. Missing from the printed version of his memoirs is his statement that he had read Schlabrendorff's memoirs *Officers Against Hitler*, in which Schlabrendorff stated that there were many informers in the prison and described what happened to Plettenberg. The surprising fact that Horstmann's account was published so long after the war, when he had been writing crime fiction under a pen name for many years, meant that there were no surviving witnesses to comment on its veracity.

It, therefore, seems very likely by that Rupprecht Gehring led the Gestapo to Plettenberg by his incautious behaviour. He was considered by everybody who met him during these last months of the war as honest in his endeavours to continue the resistance against Hitler after 20 July, but also very impulsive and reckless, which finally proved fatal for him and then for Plettenberg. What took place between Gehring and Horstmann will probably never be fully known, as we only have Horstmann's very dubious account.

The Gestapo, which until autumn-winter 1944/45 probably had insufficient evidence to arrest Plettenberg, may have been given his name by someone else, which apparently Plettenberg's interrogator Valentin told him. Gehring may, therefore, have been the one the Gestapo were able to get to talk. Their main interest in him was to get evidence of involvement of members of the House of Hohenzollern in the plans to overthrow the regime. Indeed Hitler himself had been convinced for a long time that the former Prussian royal house had played a crucial role in the conspiracy against him. Despite the fact that the Crown Prince had supported him in his presidential campaign against Hindenburg in April 1932, Hitler did not trust the former Prussian royals and saw them as potential rivals for popular support, and particularly for the support of the army.

After a conversation with the Crown Prince in August 1933 Goebbels wrote in his diary: 'The question of monarchy; they believe in their restoration. I made no pretence that it would be our greatest idiocy.' And after an evening with Hitler in January

1934: 'He is also strictly against the propaganda of the monarchists.' Later Goebbels stated that the sole achievement of the Social Democrats and the only positive outcome of the November Revolution was the elimination of the monarchy in Germany.

After the outbreak of war Hitler refused to allow the Crown Prince to rejoin the army and the remaining Prussian princes on duty at the front were not welcome, either. On 9 March 1940 Alfred Jodl, head of the Wehrmacht high command, noted in his diary after the daily military situation report with Hitler:

> The greatest outrage from the Führer when he hears that Prince Oskar leads a regiment. Schmundt was about to suggest that he should get a division, which he managed to hold in at the last moment … Hitler was so angry that he did not appear at table. His indignation was understandable, if one considers his mentality: after he had broken up all organisations which might emerge as power players in some way, in his view only the Hohenzollern princes supported by tradition could become a danger to him, should the war take an unfavourable turn. How could such a person receive military power, a regiment, or a division!

When on 26 March 1940 Prince Wilhelm, the Crown Prince's oldest son and an especial favourite of the army, died of wounds received during the French campaign, more than 50,000 mourners paid their last respects at his funeral in Potsdam. This might be called the largest spontaneous demonstration during Hitler's rule. Hitler used his death as an opportunity for the so-called 'Princes' Decree' by which all Prussian princes were withdrawn from front-line duty. From Hitler's *Table Talk* his statement dated 5 July 1942 is known: 'It would mean squandering their historical merit, if we were now to allow the Hohenzollern "spawn" influence once more, for example as officers in the Wehrmacht.' On 19 May 1943 Hitler then issued a secret order of completely removing all members of the formerly ruling princely houses from the Wehrmacht, because they 'had to be implicitly considered internationally bound'.

The active role played by the Italian royal house in Mussolini's removal in 1943 increased Hitler's fears that members of the Prussian royal house might become dangerous to him. The son-in-law of the Italian king, Prince Philipp of Hessen, although an *Obergruppenführer* in the SA, was sent to a concentration camp on suspicion of espionage, as was his wife, Princess Mafalda, who perished in August 1944 after an Allied bombing raid on Buchenwald.

According to his secretary Christa Schroeder, after 20 July 1944 Hitler declared to his entourage: 'Believe me, it will turn out that the actual instigator is the Crown Prince.' Yet this suspicion could not be substantiated by the Gestapo. Nevertheless, among other things their proximity to the Hohenzollern family was held against General Joachim von Stülpnagel and General Gottfried von Falkenhausen after 20 July during their interrogations about their involvement in the conspiracy.

Although early on the conspirators had considered appointing members of the Hohenzollern family to positions in an interim government, only a few of them, among them Carl Goerdeler, Ludwig Beck and Hans Oster, temporarily thought of restoring the monarchy. In this context both the Crown Prince and his younger son Prince Louis Ferdinand were mentioned. During the first years of the war representatives of the resistance groups held several meetings with Prince Louis Ferdinand. Goerdeler and Popitz in particular sounded out the chances of such an option, but also Klaus Bonhoeffer and Otto John arranged meetings between the prince and the union leaders Jakob Kaiser and Wilhelm Leuschner. Ulrich von Hassell even asked an American businessman in September 1941 'about the anticipated American reactions to a restoration of the monarchy' and received the answer that they would not be against it: 'Prince Louis Ferdinand would be downright popular.' Indeed the prince had gained much sympathy in the USA because he had worked on the production line at Ford in Detroit. Roosevelt had also met him several times, too.

Louis Ferdinand later reported that members of the resistance had appealed to his sense of patriotic duty to give a signal to the still undecided and hesitant army leaders as the rightful pretender to the crown. Yet he pointed out that he could not supplant his father, the Crown Prince, out of filial duty and because he did not wish to break the law of inheritance. It remains unclear whether the prince actually declined their request, because later in July 1943 he met with Otto John and his brother as well as with Albrecht Haushofer.

In any case Goerdeler advised the prince to hold himself ready at his Cadinen estate in East Prussia. The draft of a proclamation (probably not written by Goerdeler himself), which the Crown Prince was supposed to make to the army and the people in case of an overthrow of the regime, was later found among Goerdeler's papers. According to it the Crown Prince would have declared that his son Louis Ferdinand would take his place after the war.

On 20 July 1944 Louis Ferdinand was with Field Marshal Küchler in Königsberg to be briefed on the advance of the Red Army and to make preparations for the evacuation of his family from East Prussia. During his interrogation by the Gestapo at the beginning of August in Cadinen the prince managed to convince them that he had not been involved. All the conspirators had kept quiet about any contacts he may have had with them. Later Prince Louis Ferdinand said: 'It is most likely that my friends of the 20th July despite all torture did not give up my name and that I owe my escape to this loyalty of friends until death!'

Chapter 13

Prinz-Albrecht-Straße 8

On 3 March 1945, two months before the end of the war, two Gestapo officers in long leather coats arrived at Cecilienhof castle in Potsdam at around 10am and asked for Kurt von Plettenberg. He had returned the previous night from an arduous journey to Austria. In Mittelberg/Baad in the Little Walser Valley he had outlined the dramatic situation in Berlin to his employer, the Crown Prince, and discussed with him the safekeeping of the crown jewels, especially the imperial crown and Frederick the Great's gold snuffboxes, as well as other Hohenzollern family treasures, which he as general agent of the house was responsible.

The Gestapo officers arrested Plettenberg and drove him to Prinz-Albrecht-Straße in Berlin where he was detained in the Gestapo's so-called 'main prison'. Here the 'special commission 20th July' was employing 400 investigators in tracking down all those linked to the attempted *coup d'état*.

Immediately after his arrest Plettenberg's deputy, Major Müldner von Mülnheim, wrote to his wife who was in Bückeburg with the children, describing her husband's arrest.

Potsdam, 3rd March, 11am, Cecilienhof
Dear Baroness,
To my great sorrow I have to inform you today that your husband has just been arrested half an hour ago here at Cecilienhof castle by two detectives.

I must start by saying that both officers had come here already yesterday evening, when your husband was at

153

dinner with Gernlein shortly before our return from Berlin. In addition they had been here already a few days ago asking after your husband, as I was told afterwards. In any case they were announced this morning, when your husband and I were conferring in my office. Your husband then went into his office, where he received the gentlemen. After about ten minutes he asked me by telephone to join him and informed me that the two officers had arrested him. He then went with the two gentlemen to Prinz-Albrecht-Straße 8, Berlin. Your husband took along a small suitcase with warm clothes.

As it is natural, I asked Detective Inspector Valentin what this was all about, but of course received the answer that he could not tell me. Therefore I have arranged with the detective inspector that I will call on Tuesday afternoon or go to Prinz-Albrecht-Straße in person to hear more details.

I am still very much under the influence of this incident which is affecting me very deeply.

You ought to be assured, dear baroness, that we here will do everything conceivable that can be done for your husband and will keep you informed at all times.

I kiss your hand and am your humble servant,

Von Müldner

Plettenberg's staff were not aware of his work for the resistance. Nevertheless they immediately tried to get influential people involved who they believed could do something to help him. Von Müldner and privy councillor Berg, who was head of the Crown Prince's private office, drove to Berlin to see the former Reich Chancellor Franz von Papen. Von Müldner also wrote to the Minister of Finance Count Schwerin von Krosigk asking him to intervene with the head of the Reich Security Main Office, *SS-Obergruppenführer* Kaltenbrunner:

Dear Count Krosigk,

Perhaps you have the opportunity to receive the bringer of this letter, Dr Schwertfeger, Kurt Plettenberg's deputy in

Bückeburg, so that he may inform you about the steps taken by us. Beforehand I can say to my own satisfaction that the matter with Plettenberg is according to our information and impressions not as serious as we at first feared. After my meeting with you privy councillor Berg went to the Gestapo the other day and had a calmer impression of the situation from a conversation with one of the gentlemen, Detective Inspector Valentin who is also known to you …The impression and belief of all us involved (Prince Oskar, Prince Christian Schaumburg, Siebert, Berg, Schwertfeger and I) is that at the forefront of the Plettenberg case is the matter with the very unpleasant Lieutenant Gehring. In any case Plettenberg took care of this man more than he deserved and in return Gehring blabbed political things about Plettenberg, perhaps also about the house.

This is to let you know how things stand. Although I am somewhat reassured, I wish to emphasise once more how much we expect an intervention with Kaltenbrunner on your part to help us.

In haste with many regards until further notice, dear count, yours sincerely,

Müldner

Schwerin von Krosigk, therefore, turned to Göring. He later wrote in his memoirs:

My wife's cousin, Kurt Baron von Plettenberg who was especially dear to us, was only arrested in 1945. … From Göring who valued Plettenberg as an excellent hunter I received in response to my urgent call the reassuring news that nothing incriminating seemed to exist against him in person, but that he was needed for information on others …

The *Reichmarschall*'s response to Schwerin von Krosigk's intervention cannot be called anything but cynical, for Göring knew very well the methods by which the Gestapo customarily sought 'information'. That Schwerin von Krosigk was evidently content with this 'reassuring news' five days after the arrest shows the attitude by which those of his type were able to serve the Third Reich right up until the end. The Crown Prince also approached Göring but without success.

On 8 March von Müldner wrote another letter to Arianne von Plettenberg another letter, in which he signalled the all-clear:

> My dearest Baroness,
>
> ... To my joy I am today able to give you some reassurance that the matter does not seem all that serious, although we will have to be patient, of course. It is unnecessary to say that we here have immediately done everything that was somehow possible and tactically right and necessary. As a first step I straightaway went to Schwerin-Krosigk who was exceedingly nice and understanding. Dr. Schwertfeger will tell you of our various actions, which Prince Oskar and the excellent privy councillor Berg have prepared together with the lawyer Siebert and myself ... Besides rarely has a man had so many positive aspects counting for him as your husband. That finds its expression in the efforts from all sides to intervene on his behalf which we hope to direct cautiously into the right channels. It is needless to say that his personal composure was exemplary – I urgently advise against a trip here due to the practical difficulties alone. And you may rely on the fact that we will make every effort to relieve his burden and to shorten this terrible ordeal ...
>
> With many kind regards from the bottom of my heart I remain, my dear lady, yours sincerely
>
> Müldner

Privy Councillor Berg, who on 7 March had driven to Prinz-Albrecht-Straße and spoken with Valentin without learning any details or being able to speak with Plettenberg (he had brought him five apples which Valentin promised to deliver), also reassured the baroness in a letter dated 9 March: 'Some clarification has already come to pass during these last few days to the effect that Dr Schwertfeger and I were able to determine (at least everything points to this) that this is not to do with the 20th July. For your husband had nothing to do with these matters.'

Kurt von Plettenberg was among the last to be arrested in connection with the attempted *coup d'état* of 20 July 1944. Plettenberg's cell was situated in the basement of the south wing. From it he could see the prison's exercise yard with its high fence, known as the 'bear pit'. Like all thirty-eight other cells in the prison, his cell is six paces long and as wide as a man's outstretched arms. It was furnished with a pallet which he had to fold up during the day, a stool and a table fixed to the wall. In the corridor outside the cell was a waiting room with a wooden bench for the time before interrogations. A communal cell and an air-raid shelter with gas lock completed the cell block. The windows were barred and equipped with blackout screens.

The prisoners were forbidden to speak to each other, but as Fabian von Schlabrendorff later reported, time and again they were able to exchange brief messages with one another. During the heavy air raids – during Plettenberg's imprisonment there were daily attacks lasting between one and two hours – some of the prisoners and their guards had to shelter in a concrete bunker in the yard, where it was easier for them to communicate with each other, and Plettenberg exploited these opportunities himself.

Plettenberg was taken for interrogation to the fourth floor of the building where the 'special commission 20th July' had its offices. He was questioned by *Obersturmbannführer* Valentin about members of the resistance. Many of his friends and fellow conspirators had already been executed, but his closest friend, Carl-Hans von Hardenberg, and Fabian von Schlabrendorff, Karl Ludwig von und zu Guttenberg, Gotthard von Falkenhausen and Franz von Hammerstein, Kurt von Hammerstein-Equord's youngest son, were still in the hands of the Gestapo.

Nobody found out about Axel von dem Bussche who was lying in hospital gravely injured. Marion Countess Dönhoff, at that time lady of the manor at Quittainen in East Prussia, was able to avoid arrest despite being interrogated after a denunciation by her own uncle. Prince Louis Ferdinand was questioned by the Gestapo in East Prussia but they were unable to prove any link to the conspiracy. Kunrat and Ludwig, the two oldest sons of Plettenberg's friend Kurt von Hammerstein-Equord, had managed to go into hiding. Three former aides-de-camp, Ewald von Kleist-Schmenzin, Georg Sigismund von Oppen and Karl Hans Fritsche, were released by the Gestapo, but they were still being watched. Furthermore, under torture Plettenberg could have named Joachim von Willisen, Reinhild von Hardenberg (fiancée of Stauffenberg's adjutant, Werner von Haeften), Margarethe von Oven, Horst Teichgräber and many others.

Plettenberg was not going to betray anyone under any circumstances. On the seventh day of his imprisonment Valentin, encouraged by hints from informers, threatened him with 'intensified questioning' (the Gestapo euphemism for torture) unless he gave up the names of the conspirators known to him. Plettenberg was now faced with the difficult decision whether the time had come to honour his agreement with Carl-Hans von Hardenberg and commit suicide to protect his friends.

He made contact with his fellow prisoner Fabian von Schlabrendorff, who gave an account after the war of their conversation and Plettenberg's suicide:

> Declaration
>
> I, the lawyer and notary Fabian von Schlabrendorff, with office in Wiesbaden, Adelheidstraße 70, make the following statement …:
>
> During the war I met the retired chief inspector of forests Kurt Baron von Plettenberg through Carl-Hans von Hardenberg-Neuhardenberg and the late Major-General Henning von Tresckow. Our conversations were essentially about the issue of the removal of the Hitler regime by force. During these Mr von Plettenberg revealed himself to be a decided opponent of the Nazis.

On 17 August 1944 during the investigation of the attempted takeover of 20 July 1944 I was brought to ... Prinz-Albrecht-Straße.

In spring 1945, probably in March, one night I saw among the fellow prisoners also Mr von Plettenberg. At that time Berlin was attacked by Allied bombers almost every night. On these occasions certain detainees were hauled out of their cells by the Gestapo, led across the yard and sheltered in a concrete bunker during the raid. Because of this I spotted Mr von Plettenberg. I managed to make contact with him and to have a conversation. We continued these talks on several occasions, either day or night, as soon as we met outside our cells. During them Mr von Plettenberg told me that he had been denounced and that the Gestapo demanded from him the disclosure of further names from the resistance against Hitler.

One morning Mr von Plettenberg and I talked in the yard behind the cells. Mr von Plettenberg told me that he was faced with a difficult decision, as the Gestapo threatened him with coercion and torture, if he continued to refuse to give up names. Plettenberg continued that he saw no option than ending his own life, as he was not willing to meet the Gestapo's demands. I objected and begged him to postpone his decision as long as possible. At that moment of our conversation we were separated by Gestapo officers. I remained in the yard, while Mr von Plettenberg was led to his cell.

From the yard I could discern that von Plettenberg climbed up to the window of his cell to give me a sign. The sign was unmistakable. He let me know that he would try to take his own life.

Some hours later the number of the cell was called, in which Mr von Plettenberg was kept. I could hear how Gestapo officers fetched Mr von Plettenberg for questioning on one of the upper floors. Shortly after, a strange noise was heard. I looked out of the window of my cell and saw Mr

Plettenberg lying almost in front of my window. He no longer showed any sign of life. A few minutes later Gestapo officers appeared and carried Mr von Plettenberg's corpse out of the yard. During this they told each other that in response to the intimation by the Gestapo that force would now be used against him, should he continue to refuse, Mr von Plettenberg punched one of the senior officers on the jaw, climbed onto the windowsill and threw himself down into the yard.

I recount the event in the manner it has committed itself indelibly to my memory.

Wiesbaden, 11th September 1957
Signed Fabian von Schlabrendorff

Further insights into the events are given in a letter by Berg. He informed the Crown Prince about the details some days after the sad incident, as far as they had been reported to him by Valentin:

Private and confidential! Potsdam, 15th March 1945
To His Imperial Highness, the Crown Prince

Mittelberg-Baad

Your Imperial Highness,
Subsequent to yesterday's telegram by His Royal Highness Prince Oskar I wish to report the following:

Yesterday around noon I was called urgently to Berlin by the interrogating detective inspector, Mr Valentin. There he disclosed the following to me: President Baron von Plettenberg took his own life on Saturday, 10th March, at 11:30am. He threw himself out of a window. The autopsy findings were read to me in part: double cranial fracture, fragmentation of the right or left chest area with internal bleeding. Death seems to have been instant.

I received the following tasks: notification of the wife and the employer, further to His Royal Highness Prince Oskar and His Excellency von Müldner. In addition no notification is to be made. If questioned we may say to the staff that President Baron von Plettenberg had suddenly deceased on Saturday, 10th March; nothing more.

The corpse has been released and can be buried at any site chosen. This is probably going to be the Bornstedt cemetery.

The funeral has to be a modest, private affair. Only three to four wreaths may be laid down. A clergyman may be involved. The Gestapo has to be informed of the time and place of the funeral 24 hours in advance. Outsiders may not be informed, in particular about the time and place of the funeral service. I cannot and must not say more, for I have been ordered to secrecy, and any transgression of the constraints put on me will have consequences involving the state police. I therefore urgently request you not to say anything about the contents of this letter to any outsider. ...

At today's placing in the coffin I will put a bouquet of flowers from Your Imperial Highnesses.

Your most humble servant ...

Berg was also present when Plettenberg's body was put in his coffin. He describes his impressions to the Crown Prince in a letter later sent to Mittelberg-Baad:

I have taken part ... in ... Baron von Plettenberg's placing in the coffin on 15th march. Initially I was worried that I would find an unrecognisable corpse. I have to say that the deceased has been placed in the coffin with a very peaceful expression and completely recognisable. He had a bruise on the left side of his head and bruises on his chest. Besides the flowers of his widow I placed those of Your Imperial Highnesses in the coffin, and in addition a bouquet of forest flowers from the staff. The next day His Excellency von Müldner conveyed the deceased from Berlin to Potsdam ...

161

Kurt von Plettenberg was buried on 17 March 1945 in the Bornstedt cemetery in Potsdam. His predecessor, General von Dommes, had asked the Bornstedt parish office for a plot on behalf of the general management of the former Prussian royal house, pointing out that the 'suddenly passed away general agent' had been responsible for all the assets of the Prussian royal house, thus also for Bornstedt.

The strict requirements of the Gestapo were met. The funeral service was conducted by the son of the court chaplain, Bruno Doehring, who in 1941 had also given the eulogy for Emperor Wilhelm II in Doorn. Berg wrote about this in a later letter to the Crown Prince dated 26 march 1945: 'The eulogy of court chaplain Doehring was more than brief. President Baron von Plettenberg would have deserved a better one. Yet formalities do not matter. The mortal remains have found a good place and he himself will probably have watched – smiling as usual – this poor sinner's burial from above ...'

News of Plettenberg's death spread quickly despite measures taken by the Gestapo. Prince Oskar of Prussia, at that time substituting for his brother as Plettenberg's point of contact in matters of the Hohenzollern family, wrote to his sister, Duchess Victoria Luise of Braunschweig-Lüneburg, and identically to his brothers:

'Today it is my sad duty to give you the shocking news that President Baron von Plettenberg, so admired by us all – after he was taken away for questioning on 3rd March – has passed away on 10th March according to the office responsible. His work was his life and he had no enemies.'

Arianne von Plettenberg only learned of her husband's death on 16 March in Bückeburg. The telephone lines from Berlin had been disrupted for days. Arianne's mother, Freda von Maltzahn, noted in her diary:

16th March 1945; in the evening the prince [Wolrad von Schaumburg-Lippe] and Dr Schwertfeger [legal advisor of the court chamber] came and brought Nanni the unbelievable news that Kurdel had died in Berlin and that the funeral would be the next day at the Bornstedt cemetery. Ivonne [von Kuenheim, née Countess Dönhoff] and Marion [Countess Dönhoff who meanwhile had reached Bückeburg after her escape from East Prussia] later came as well and together we tried to cope with this sorrow.

17th March 1945; very early Nanni received letters by messengers from Prince Oskar and the gentlemen from Potsdam. I cannot put down details on paper. It is all so grave and so overwhelming! Nanni is beyond description in her pain and her composure. Ivonne Kuenheim, the prince, Marion … were here and brought … flowers …

The authority for moving the corpse from the Berlin police president was issued by the 3rd Police District under the reference 3R.9290 dated 16 March 1945, thus six days after the death.

Authority to move the corpse.
The corpse placed in the coffin according to regulations of the 54-year-old Kurt Baron von Plettenberg, who died on 10th March 1945 in Berlin, Prinz-Albrecht-Straße 8 by suicide, shall be conveyed by train from Berlin via Wannsee to Potsdam for interment. For this conveyance of the corpse the permission has been granted.
Signature of the district director; administrative fee – 1 Reichsmark.

Arianne von Plettenberg could not travel to Berlin from Bückeburg in time for the funeral at such short notice. Only days later, was she able to learn the details of her husband's death from a letter sent by Berg on 16 March. He wrote: 'I am able to tell you, my dearest baroness, that the departed has been placed into the coffin with a peaceful expression. I have placed red tulips (other, white flowers were unfortunately not available) in his hands as your last farewell, further a bouquet from Their Imperial Highnesses and a bunch of forest flowers from the staff.' The high regard which Berg – and Plettenberg's other colleagues – had for the deceased was also expressed in this letter.

A few days later Berg informed the widow that her husband 'left some lines in his cell, which however will not reach our hands. I have learned of them confidentially. They contain even in this last hour the request to take care of you and thanks for the friendly treatment in Prinz-Albrecht-Straße, still showing his kindness and his goodness to the very end. Perhaps later I will be able to say more, but now I am not permitted to do so.' Yet the farewell letter was never handed to the widow. Berg later quoted a few lines from memory to her: 'I do not fear death, for I will have a fair judge. Will my family be provided for? Please give the apple and the cigarettes still in my possession to the guard who always was so kind to me.'

In *Thoughts are Strength* by the architect Werner March, which it is said Kurt von Plettenberg read every day, the wording of an old Viennese inscription on a bridge is found under the date of his death: 'Death is life – dying a gate – everything is only transition.'

Epilogue

'Greater love hath no man than this,
that a man lay down his life for his friends'

Kurt von Plettenberg's grave is in Bornstedt cemetery in Potsdam, burial place of many personalities from Prussia's history, including the famous court gardeners Peter Joseph Lenné and Gottfried Sello, the architect Friedrich Ludwig Persius, and the General and Prussian Minister of War Erich von Falkenhayn, on whose family plot a memorial stone for his son-in-law Henning von Tresckow has also been erected.

Kurt von Plettenberg's tombstone bears the inscription: 'He gave his life for his friends in the resistance of the 20th July 1944.' A letter written by Fabian von Schlabrendorff to Plettenberg's widow on 8 January 1946, reads:

> I will never forget the proud self-possession with which your husband told me of his decision. He was smiling. His composure was unbroken. He reminded me of a cavalier of the old school. During my time of imprisonment I have seen many people going to their deaths, and most of them remained solemn and dignified. Your husband went beyond that. Free and smiling he made the decision, in order to preserve his friends and family, to end his own life. With the same attitude he carried out his resolution.

To the reasons given by Schlabrendorff for his suicide, namely the preservation of his family and friends, Plettenberg's youngest daughter has added that her father chose suicide for the sake of his own dignity as well. Self-respect, in the former social world from which he came was of very great value. It guided him as much as the strong belief that he would become close to God by his death.

Originally only a wooden cross erected by Kurt von Plettenberg's staff on 31 January 1946, his 55th birthday, marked the grave. Words from the Gospel of John (chapter 15, verse 13) were inscribed on it: 'Greater love hath no man than this, that a man lay down his life for his friends.'

The legal advisor of the court chamber, Dr. Schwertfeger, gave a commemorative speech in which he recalled once more the events surrounding Plettenberg's death and concluded:

> In this manner Baron von Plettenberg stands before our very eyes as the embodiment of the bible quotation on his cross – as a knight in shining armour. Way beyond the circle of his family and friends his death is an irreplaceable loss. Men like him are desperately needed in for the rebuilding of our downtrodden fatherland. We, his old colleagues, are glad that he was one of us and counted among our closest circle of comrades. We will not forget him.

In 1989 – even before the reunification of Germany – instead of the wooden cross a tombstone based on his children's design was erected. Only after the fall of the Berlin Wall was the family able to care for the grave in the Bornstedt cemetery themselves. Many visitors to the Bornstedt cemetery are touched that the old wooden cross is still kept by the parish in the 'martyrs' corner' of the chapel.

Kurt von Plettenberg has also been officially commemorated on several occasions. At the German Resistance memorial in Berlin, a photograph and biography of him can be found in the gallery of the men and women of the 20th July. Also in the exhibition commemorating the 20th July, which some time ago was opened in the old barracks of IR 9 in Potsdam, he is represented with his biography. At Cecilienhof castle and Neuhardenberg castle he is also commemorated by exhibition panels.

In his hometown of Bückeburg a commemorative plaque has been mounted at the court pharmacy, the former residence of his family. In Potsdam a street was named after him in the Jägervorstadt, likewise in Hannover-Wettbergen and in Hamburg-Bergedorf where the Senate of the Free and Hansa City saw to this honour at the suggestion of the Federal Office for Forest and Wood Management resident there. Also in Plettenberg, the Westfalian town of his ancestors, a road was named in his honour on 10 March 2015.

Many people who got to know him well have been unable to forget him. They appreciated his personality and his dedication, for example Marion Dönhoff. In the last years of her life she erected a memorial in honour of her friends from the resistance of 20 July 1944 at Crottorf Castle in Bergisches Land. Among the six names which she had engraved on the pedestal of a sculpture by Alexander Libermann, Kurt von Plettenberg's name can be found.

Axel von dem Bussche said in a memorial address on 28 April 1985: 'I have to thank Kurt von Plettenberg because he has taught me without lecturing what is important in life: a blessed sense of proportion and perspective, harmony and balance.'

Siegfried Count zu Eulenburg, the last commander of the 1st Foot Guards wrote in 1950 in memory of a visit by Plettenberg to his widow:

> It was a melancholy pleasure to me to relive the wonderful days whose complete success was not the least due to Kurt's exceptional personality. Like few people he always knew how to unite seriousness with serenity. He was like a son to me and until the end of my life will stand before my eyes as the embodiment of a noble man.

Prince Louis Ferdinand also publicly expressed his gratitude to Kurt von Plettenberg in 1991 on the occasion of naming a museum train in Bruchhausen-Vilsen 'Plettenberg'. A report of the event reads:

> Dr Louis Ferdinand expressed his pleasure about being allowed to name a locomotive of the museum railway 'Plettenberg'. The name Plettenberg means a lot to him, for an employee of his family named Plettenberg chose suicide because of the expected torture after the assassination attempt on Hitler and thus saved the life of His Imperial Highness.

His friend Carl-Hans von Hardenberg mourned him with the words: 'There has hardly been any nobler man than Kurtel Plettenberg. His loss is never-ending. '

Acknowledgements

The suggestion to write a biography of Kurt von Plettenberg sprang from his children Dorothea-Marion von Plettenberg and Karl-Wilhelm von Plettenberg. Both made a major contribution to the completion of the book. They permitted me to consult the extensive family archive, supported me in my research and participated in the editing of the manuscript. Without their continuous critical collaboration this book could not have come about. Therefore I am particularly indebted to them.

I furthermore owe thanks to all those who also supported my research, especially the Berlin military historian Klaus Mayer; the forest engineer Dr. Andreas Gautschi and the retired forester Dr. Albrecht Milnik, Eberswalde. Rüdiger von Voss and Dr. Christoph Studt have to be thanked for their critical review of the manuscript and their many suggestions.

For access to the papers of General von Dommes, Major Müldner von Mülnheim and Privy Councillor Arthur Berg as well as to the files of the general management of the former Prussian royal house I am indebted to the director of the secret state archive Prussian cultural heritage in Berlin-Dahlem, Prof. Dr. Jürgen Kloosterhuis.

Carmen Lorenz and I. Matschke of the Federal Archive in Berlin kindly supported me, too. The same holds true for Dr. Andreas Sander of the library of the Topography of Terror Foundation.

ACKNOWLEDGEMENTS

I was helped along by the references provided by Heide Langguth and Dr. Reiner Dorner after reading the first draft of the manuscript. Finally my heartfelt thanks go to my editor at the F.A. Herbig publishing house, Dagmar von Keller, for her valuable work on the text.

Timeline

of Kurt Freiherr von Plettenberg

31 January 1891
Born in Bückeburg, second son of Karl Baron von Plettenberg and his wife Clara née Countess von Wedel.

1897
Enrolment at school.

1900–10
Attendance at grammar schools in Potsdam, Charlottenburg and Kassel.

26 February 1910
Abitur in Kassel.

1910 – 1911
Two semesters of studying law at the universities of Kiel and Lausanne.

1 March 1911 – 30 September 1911
Forestry apprentice at the Prussian State forest district of Menz (Ruppin).

1 October 1911 – 30 September 1912
Military service with the 18th (2nd Grand Ducal Mecklenburgian) Dragoon Regiment in Parchim.

1 October 1912 – 1 August 1914
Continuation of studies at the Forestry Academy in Hannoversch-Münden. After three terms: preliminary examination in forestry (21 March 1914). Fourth term interrupted by outbreak of war.

1 August 1914
Call-up to military service as reserve lieutenant in the 2nd Guard Uhlan Regiment at the Western Front.

30 August 1914
Death of his brother Karl-Wilhelm near St. Quentin

1 May 1915
Leader of the regiment's newly-formed cavalry machine-gun detachment.

1 June 1916
Transfer to IR 408 on the Eastern Front.

November 1917
Leader of a machine-gun company in the regiment.

April 1918 – 7 November 1918
Machine-gun officer with the 1st Foot Guards on the Western Front.

20 December 1918
Discharge from military service; decorations: Iron Cross 1st and 2nd Class, the Knight's Cross with Swords of the Saxon Albrecht Order and the Medal of Merit of Schaumburg-Lippe.

December 1918 – June 1919
Continuation of studies in law at the University of Berlin and in forestry at the University of Munich.

27 June 1919
Passes 1st state examination (junior forester).

7 July 1919 – 20 June 1920
Position of junior forester in the East Prussian forest district
Rothebude in the government district of Gumbinnen.

21 June 1920 – 11 May 1921
Traveling junior forester in East Prussia, Silesia and Eberswalde.

11 May 1921
Graduation at the Academy of Forestry Hannoversch-Münden as
assessor.

19 May 1921 – 31 March 1923
Director of the timber trade department of the Stralsund
government as State Senior Forester.

1 May 1923 – 31 March 1930
Manager of Count Dönhoff's forests in Friedrichstein near
Königsberg.

April 1930
Head of the forestry department of the Berlin-Brandenburg
chamber of agriculture.

1 June 1931
Promotion to head forester.

15 October 1932
In addition: provisional appointment at the Reich Ministry of Food.

1934
Budget consultant of the Prussian State Forestry administration and
acceptance as State Head Forester into the Reich Forestry Office.

9 September 1934
Marriage Arianne Baroness of Maltzahn from Schossow in
Pomerania.

19 December 1936
Birth of daughter Christa-Erika in Berlin.

1 October 1937
Termination of employment at the Reich State Forestry Office; acceptance of property management of the Princely House of Schaumburg-Lippe as president of the court chamber.

23 March 1938
Birth of son Karl-Wilhelm in Bückeburg.

10 February & 5 June 1938
Death of parents.

26 August 1939
Call-up as major reserve major IR 9 in the 23rd Division; participation in the military in Poland.

30 September 1939 – 22 June 1940
As aide-de-camp (IIa) at the regimental staff of the 23rd Division on the Western Front in France.

3 July 1940 – February 1941
Command of the 3rd Battalion of IR 9 as major; from October deployment on the Eastern Front as part of 123rd Division.

8 May 1941
Command of the reserve battalion of IR 9 in Potsdam.

5 July 1941
Command of the 3rd Battalion of IR 415 on the Eastern Front; from October commander of IR 415 in the 123rd Division; German Cross in Gold, Silver Clasp to the Iron Cross First Class, Infantry Assault Badge and Badge of the Wounded.

22 November 1941
Leave to conduct affairs as president of the court chamber in Bückeburg.
1 January 1942
Appointment as general agent of the former Prussian royal house.

1942–1944
Participation in the plans for the 20 July 1944 in the circle around Hardenberg, Stauffenberg and Tresckow

25 March 1942
Transfer to the 338th Infantry Battalion in Crossen/ Oder; from June deferred from military service.

15 October 1943
Birth of daughter Dorothea-Marion in Bückeburg.

11 August 1944
Rejection of request to return to the army by the general command of Third Army due to age.

3 March 1945
Arrest by the Gestapo; detained in the Gestapo prison at Prinz-Albrecht-Straße 8, Berlin.

10 March 1945
Kurt von Plettenberg's suicide by jumping from the fourth floor of the interrogation block.

17 March 1945 Funeral at the Bornstedt cemetery in Potsdam.

Bibliography and Sources

Biographies

Dönhoff, Marion Gräfin, *Kurt Freiherr von Plettenberg. Briefe 1928–1945*, ed. Hermann Graf Hatzfeldt and Dorothea-Marion Freifrau von Plettenberg (Privately printed, 2009).

Hilf, Hans Hugo, 'Dem Gedächtnis an Kurt Freiherr von Plettenberg (1891–1945)', special print from *Forstarchiv* Vol. 30, No. 7 (15 July 1959), pp. 133–4.

Keil, Lars-Broder, 'Kurt Freiherr von Plettenberg (1891–1945)', in Vollmer, Antje, and Keil, Lars-Broder (eds), *Stauffenbergs Gefährten. Das Schicksal der unbekannten Verschwörer* (Berlin, 2013), pp. 137–53.

Plettenberg, Dorothea von, 'Kurt Freiherr von Plettenberg', in *Bückeburger im Widerstand. Dokumentation zur Erinnerungsfeier* (9 October 2008).

Plettenberg, Karl-Wilhelm Freiherr von, 'Kurt Freiherr von Plettenberg, Loyalität und Menschlichkeit im Widerstand', in Schaumburger Landschaft (ed), *Gegen den Strom. Widerstand und Zivilcourage im Nationalsozialismus in Schaumburg* (Bielefeld 2005), pp. 89–104 (contains among other things Marion Countess Dönhoff's memories of Kurt von Plettenberg recorded in 1985)

Unpublished presentations and commemorative addresses

Bussche, Axel von dem, 'Zur Erinnerung an Kurt von Plettenberg', commemorative address, Bückeburg, 28 April 1985; excerpts from this in Bussche, Axel von dem, 'Zur Erinnerung an Kurt von Plettenberg', in Mühlen, Bengt von zur (ed.), *Die Angeklagten des 20. Juli vor dem Volksgerichtshof* (Berlin, 2001), pp. 112–15.

Reich, Ines, 'Kurt Freiherr von Plettenberg. Ambivalenzen einer Biographie'; presentation at Potsdam, 18 July 1997.

Plettenberg, Karl-Wilhelm von, 'Zur Erinnerung an Kurt Freiherr von Plettenberg (1891–1945)'; presentation on the occasion of the 20 July 1944 memorial in Potsdam on 19 July 2012; see http://www.preußen.de/de/heute/forum_preussen.html, 15 August 2012.

Plettenberg, Dorothea von, 'Kurt Freiherr von Plettenberg', on the occasion of the commemoration of four citizens of Bückeburg who stood up to the regime during the Nazi period, Bückeburg, n.d.

Schmidt, Eberhard, 'Kurt von Plettenberg und sein Widerstand gegen das "Dritte Reich"', presentation at the meeting of the research foundation 20th July 1944, Königswinter 22–24 February 2012.

Sources

This biography is largely based on the von Plettenberg family archive, in which Kurt von Plettenberg's diaries, letters and parts of the official correspondence can be found. Unfortunately the correspondence between husband and wife has been lost in the chaos of the post-war years apart from a few letters. The same holds true for the diaries after 1934.

In addition files of the Secret Archive Prussian Cultural Heritage in Berlin-Dahlem, of the Federal Archive Berlin and of the Wehrmacht Inquiries Office were used as well as material from the German Resistance Memorial Centre and the library of the 'Topography of Terror' foundation, Berlin.

Preface: 'I do not fear death, for I will have a fair judge.'

For the telephone call:

Hardenberg, Carl-Hans von, *Ein deutsches Schicksal im Widerstand*, ed. Günter Agde (Berlin, 1994), p. 49.

The quotation from Eberhard Zeller:

Zeller, Eberhard, *Geist der Freiheit. Der Zwanzigste Juli* (Munich, 1965), p. 457.

Chapter 1: The Prussian Heritage

For the genealogy of the von Plettenberg family:

Genealogisches Handbuch des Adels, edited by the Deutsches Adelsarchiv, vol. 119, Freiherrliche Häuser, Vol. X (Limburg a.d. Lahn 1999), pp. 421–3.

Plettenberg, General Karl von, *Lebenserinnerungen* (300 pages of manuscript) unpublished, Plettenberg family archive.

Schulte-Kramer, Friedrich, *Das Rittergut Stockum, Sundener Heimatblätter* (18th series, 2010), pp. 12–14.

For the nobility's role in the transition to modernity and for 'nobility':

Funck, Marcus, 'Vom Höfling zum soldatischen Mann' in Conze, Eckart, and Wienfort, Monika (eds), *Adel und Moderne. Deutschland im europäischen Vergleich im 19. und 20. Jahrhundert* (Cologne, 2004), pp. 205–36.

Malinowski, Stephan, *Vom König zum Führer. Sozialer Niedergang und politische Radikalisierung im deutschen Adel zwischen Kaiserreich und NS-Staat* (Berlin, 2003), pp. 47–117 (quotation from Kleist-Schmenzin: p. 80).

Stonemann, Marc B., 'Bürgerliche und adelige Krieger. Zum Verhältnis von sozialer Herkunft und Berufskultur in der wilhelminischen Armee', in Reif, Heinz (ed.), *Adel und Bürgertum in Deutschland*, Vol. II (Berlin, 2001), pp. 25–63.

Wehler, Hans Ulrich, *Deutsche Gesellschaftsgeschichte*, Vol. 3, 1845/49–1914 (Munich, 1995).

Wienfort, Monika, *Adel in der Moderne* (Göttingen, 2006).

For the history of Prussia and its values:

Dönhoff, Marion Gräfin, *Preußen – Maß und Maßlosigkeit* (Berlin, 1987).

Haffner, Sebastian, *Preußen ohne Legende* (Hamburg, 1978).

Kroll, Frank-Lothar, *Die Hohenzollern* (Munich, 2008).

_____, 'Sehnsüchte nach Preußen', in Schoeps, Julius H. (ed.), *Preußen. Geschichte eines Mythos* (Berlin-Brandenburg, 2000), pp. 220–5.

Schoeps, Hans Joachim, *Die Ehre Preußens* (Stuttgart, 1951).

For the history of forestry in Prussia and the Mounted Feldjäger Corps:

Koehler, Wolfgang, *Geschichte des Feldjägervereins und der Akademischen Feldjägergesellschaft 1914-1945* (Göttingen, 1986).

Theilemann, Wolfram G., *Adel im Grünen Rock. Adeliges Jägertum, Großprivatwaldbesitz und die preußische Forstbeamtenschaft 1866-1914* (Berlin, 2004), pp. 203ff.

For the decision to choose boxing instead of a fencing fraternity:

Bottlenberg-Landsberg, Maria Theodora von dem, *Karl Ludwig Freiherr von und zu Guttenberg 1902-1945. Ein Lebensbild* (Berlin 2003, p189

Chapter 2: Lieutenant in the First World War

For the causes and course of the First World War:

Ulrich, Volker, *Die nervöse Großmacht 1871-1918. Aufstieg und Untergang des deutschen Kaiserreichs* (Frankfurt/M., 2007), pp. 407–573.

Stevenson, David, *1914-1918. Der Erste Weltkrieg* (Düsseldorf, 2006).

Wehler, Hans Ulrich, *Deutsche Gesellschaftsgeschichte*, Vol. 4, 1914-1949 (Munich 2003), s.a. pp. 14ff.

For the Langemark myth:

Studt, Christoph, 'Langemark – Mythos in Stein. Die Deutschen und der Erste Weltkrieg', *Verein Alter Dyonisianer. Rheine a.d. Ems* bulletin No. LVII (June 1995), pp. 19–33.

For General Karl von Plettenberg:

Plettenberg, General Karl von, *Lebenserinnerungen* (300 pages of manuscript), unpublished, Plettenberg family archive.

Chapter 3: Difficult Years

For the aristocracy's reaction to the collapse of the empire:

Funck, Marcus, 'Schock und Chance. Der deutsche Militäradel in der Weimarer Republik zwischen Stand und Profession', in Reif, Heinz (ed.), *Adel und Bürgertum in Deutschland, vol. 2, Entwicklungslinien und Wendepunkte im 20. Jahrhundert* (Berlin 2001).

Malinowski, Stephan, *Vom König zum Führer. Sozialer Niedergang und politische Radikalisierung im deutschen Adel zwischen Kaiserreich und NS-Staat* (Berlin, 2003), pp. 198–291, 321–421.

Meteling, Wencke, 'Der deutsche Zusammenbruch 1918 in den Selbstzeugnissen adeliger preußischer Offiziere', in Conze, Eckart, and Wienfort, Monika (eds), *Adel und Moderne. Deutschland im europäischen Vergleich im 19. Und 20. Jahrhundert* (Cologne, 2004), pp. 289–321 (quote from Loringhoven: p. 318).

For the history of the Weimar Republic:

Mommsen, Hans, *Aufstieg und Untergang der Republik von Weimar. 1918 – 1933* (Berlin, 1998).

Kolb, Eberhard, *Die Weimarer Republik* (Munich, 2002).

Wehler, Hans-Ulrich, *Deutsche Gesellschaftsgeschichte, Vol. 4, 1914–1949* (Munich, 2003).

For the history of forestry:

Rubner, Heinrich, *Deutsche Forstgeschichte 1933-1945* (St. Katharinen, 1985), Chapter 1.

Theilemann, Wolfram G., *Adel im Grünen Rock. Adliges Jägertum,*

Großprivatwaldbesitz und die preußische Forstbeamtenschaft 1866 – 1914 (Berlin, 2004).

Chapter 4: Marion Countess Dönhoff

Excerpts from correspondence between Marion Gräfin Dönhoff and Kurt Baron von Plettenberg:

Hatzfeld, Hermann Graf, and Plettenberg, Dorothea-Marion Freifrau von (eds), *Briefe 1928-1945. Marion Gräfin Dönhoff – Kurt Freiherr von Plettenberg* (Private publication, 2009).

For the Dönhoff family, Friedrichstein castle and East Prussia before 1945:

Dohna-Schlobitten, Alexander Fürst zu, *Erinnerungen eines alten Ostpreußen* (Leer, 2006), pp. 161ff.

Dönhoff, Friedrich Graf, *'Die Welt ist so, wie man sie sieht'. Erinnerungen an Marion Dönhoff* (Hamburg, 2004).

Dönhoff, Marion Gräfin, *Entstehung und Bewirtschaftung eines ostdeutschen Großbetriebes. Die Friedrichstein-Güter von der Ordenszeit bis zur Bauernbefreiung* (dissertation, Basel University, 1935)

_____, *Kindheit in Ostpreußen* (Berlin, 1988).

_____, *Um der Ehre Willen. Erinnerungen an die Freunde vom 20. Juli* (Berlin, 1994).

_____, *Namen, die keiner mehr nennt. Ostpreußen – Menschen und Geschichten* (Reinbek, 2009).

_____, *Bilder, die langsam verblassen. Ostpreußische Erinnerungen* (Würzburg, 2007), pp. 145–8.

Harprecht, Klaus, *Die Gräfin. Marion Dönhoff. Eine Biographie* (Reinbek, 2008).

Heck, Kilian, and Thielemann, Christian, *Friedrichstein. Das Schloss der Dönhoffs in Ostpreußen* (Berlin and Munich 2006), p. 76.

Kuenheim, Haug von, *Marion Dönhoff* (Reinbek, 1999), preface.

Lehndorff, Hans Graf von, *Ostpreußisches Tagebuch* (Munich, 1997).

Chapter 5: Hopes for the 'Third Reich'

For the end of the Weimar Republic and the rise of National Socialism:

'Aufruf der Reichsregierung vom 31. Januar 1933', in Jacobsen, Hans-Adolf, and Jochmann, Werner (eds), *Ausgewählte Dokumente zur Geschichte des Nationalsozialismus, 1933-1945*, Vol. 2 (Bielefeld, 1961), document 31.1.1933.

Bracher, Karl-Dietrich, *Die nationalsozialistische Machtergreifung. Studien zur Errichtung des totalitären Herrschaftssystems in Deutschland 1933-34* (Cologne, 1962).

Herbert, Ulrich, 'Wer waren die Nationalsozialisten. Typologien politischen Verhaltens im NS-Staat', in Hirschfeld, Gerhard, and Jesak, Tobias (eds), *Karrieren im Nationalsozialismus* (Frankfurt/M. and New York, 2004), pp. 17–42.

Pufendorf, Astrid von, *Die Plancks* (Berlin, 2006), pp. 135, 159ff.

Winkler, Heinrich August, *Weimar 1918-1933. Die Geschichte der ersten deutschen Demokratie* (Munich, 1993).

Quotation by Lutz Graf Schwerin von Krosigk:

Diary, entry dated 5 February 1933, in Schwerin von Krosigk, Lutz Graf, *Staatsbankrott* (Göttingen, 1974), p. 166.

For the Protestant church under the Nazi regime:

Brakelmann, Günter, *Evangelische Kirche im Entscheidungsjahr 1933/34: Der Weg nach Barmen* (Berlin, 2010).

_____, 'Nationalprotestantismus und Nationalsozialismus' in Jansen, Christian, Niethammer, Lutz, and Weisbrod, Bernd (eds), *Von der Aufgabe der Freiheit. Festschrift für Hans Mommsen zum 5 November 1995* (Berlin, 1995), pp. 337–50.

Jähnichen, Traugott, 'Selbstbehauptung – Protest – Widerstand. Zum Verhalten der Bekennenden Kirche gegenüber dem Nationalsozialismus', in Brakelmann, Günter, and Keller, Manfred, *Der 20. Juli und das Erbe des Deutschen Widerstandes* (Münster, 2005), pp. 40–61.

Wehler, Hans-Ulrich, *Deutsche Gesellschaftsgeschichte*, vol. 4, 1914-1949 (Munich, 2003), pp. 795–818.

For the conflict regarding *Gleischaltung*:

Koehler, Wolfgang, *Geschichte des Feldjägervereins und der Akademischen Feldjägergesellschaften 1914-1945* (Göttingen, 1986), pp. 191–6.

Chapter 6: Arianne Baroness von Maltzahn

For Kurt von Plettenberg's relations to the Hardenbergs and to the von Maltzahn family:

Hardenberg, Carl-Hans von, *Ein deutsches Schicksal im Widerstand*, ed. Günter Agde (Berlin, 1994), pp. 120–59.

Hardenberg, Reinhild Gräfin von, *Auf immer neuen Wegen. Erinnerungen an Neuhardenberg und den Widerstand gegen den Nationalsozialismus* (Berlin, 2003), pp. 70–8.

Letters and diary accounts by Arianne Baroness von Maltzahn and Freda von Maltzahn from the Plettenberg family archive

Chapter 7: Resignation from Public Service

For Plettenberg's position in the Agricultural Chamber Berlin-Brandenburg and in the Reich Ministry of Food:

Federal Archive Berlin: file holdings on the Reich Forestry Office (R3701).

Hilf, Hans Hugo, 'Zum Gedächtnis an Kurt Freiherr von Plettenberg (1891-1945)', *Forstarchiv* Vol. 30, No. 7 (15 July 1959), pp. 133ff.

Milnik, Albrecht, 'Kurt Freiherr von Plettenberg' in *ibid., Im Dienst am Wald. Lebenswege und Leistungen brandenburgischer Forstleute* (Remagen-Oberwinter, 2006), pp. 314ff.

Personal correspondence from 21 January 1931 to 19 November 1934 (two file folders) in the Plettenberg family archive.

For the development of forestry during the Third Reich:

Gautschi, Andreas, *Der Reichsjägermeister. Fakten und Legenden um Hermann Göring* (Melsungen, 2006), pp. 60–8 (on Plettenberg: p. 65).

Petzina, Ditemar, *Autarkiepolitik im Dritten Reich* (Stuttgart, 1968).

Radkau, Joachim, and Uekötter, Frank (eds), *Naturschutz und Nationalsozialismus* (Frankfurt and New York, 2003).

Rubner, Heinrich, *Deutsche Forstgeschichte 1933-1945* (St. Katharinen, 1985, 1997), pp. 24–31, 54ff, 64–75, 94–107 (on Plettenberg: p. 293).

Plettenberg's remark on his refusal to take part in the destruction of the German forests is attested by a written note by Jan von Ledebur, son of Kurt von Plettenberg's sister, to Dorothea von Plettenberg dated 13 October 2011.

For Plettenberg's role at the princely court chamber of Schaumburg-Lippe:

Correspondence of the president from 8 October 1937 to 24 February 1945 (six file folders) and further files concerning the representation of private forest owners (1938-1942) as well as files on his activity in the committee for forestry policy of the German Forestry Association (1939–41) in the Plettenberg family archive

Chapter 8: Infantry Regiment 9

For Hitler's war aims and the course of the Second World War:

Benz, Wolfgang (ed.), *Handbuch der deutschen Geschichte, 20. Jahrhundert*, Vol. 4 (Stuttgart 2004).

Broszat, Martin, and Schwabe, Klaus (eds), *Die deutschen Eliten und der Weg in den Zweiten Weltkrieg* (Munich, 1989).

Die Wehrmachtsberichte 1939-1945, Vol. 3, 1 January 1944 – 9 May 1945 (Munich, 1985).

Müller, Rolf-Dieter, *Der letzte deutsche Krieg 1939-1945* (Stuttgart, 2005).

For the Potsdam Infantry Regiment 9:

Finker, Kurt,' Das Potsdamer Infanterieregiment 9 und der konservativ militärische Widerstand' in Kroener, Bernhard R. (ed), *Potsdam. Staat, Armee, Residenz* (Berlin, 1993).

Heinemann, Ulrich, *Ein konservativer Rebell. Fritz-Dietlof Graf von der Schulenburg und der 20. Juli* (Berlin, 1990).

Jürgen, and Steinbach, Peter (eds), *Der Widerstand gegen den Nationalsozialismus* (Munich and Zurich, 1985), pp. 533–45.

Klausa, Ekkehard, 'Preußische Soldatentradition und Widerstand. Das Potsdamer Infanterieregiment 9 zwischen "Tag von Potsdam" und 20. Juli 1944', in Schmädeke, Jurgen, and Steinbach,Peter (eds), *Der Widerstand gegen den Nationalsozialismus* (Munich and Zurich, 1985), pp. 533–45.

Krug, Paul, 'Rückschau auf Potsdam und Friedensjahre im 9. (Preuß.) Infanterie-Regiment', in Medem, Gevinon von (ed.), *Axel von dem Bussche* (Mainz, 1994), pp. 11–29.

Nayhauß-Cormons, Mainhardt Graf von, *Zwischen Gehorsam und Gewissen. Richard von Weizsäcker und das Infanterie-Regiment 9* (Bergisch-Gladbach, 1994), pp. 283–90, 371, 403

Paul, Wolfgang, *Das Potsdamer Infanterieregiment Nr. 9, 1918-1945*, 2 vols (Osnabrück, 1983), text volume, pp 544–9 (for Plettenberg: pp. 152, 169).

Reich, Ines, *Potsdam und der 20. Juli 1944* (Freiburg, 1994).

Schmädecke, Jürgen, and Steinbach, Peter (eds), *Der Widerstand gegen den Nationalsozialismus* (Munich and Zurich, 1985), pp. 533–45.

For the report on the mass shootings in Dubno:

Krall, Hanna, 'Phantomschmerz' in Medem, Gevinon von (ed), *Axel von dem Bussche* (Mainz, 1994), pp. 230ff.

A copy of the article by Werner Spiegel, *Der unverwundbare Major*, can be found in the Plettenberg family archive (undated).

Chapter 9: In the Service of the Hohenzollerns
For Kurt von Plettenberg's appointment as general agent of the former Prussian royal house and for his activities: see file stock general

administration former Prussian royal house in the secret state archive Prussian cultural heritage, Berlin-Dahlem (1. HA Rep 100a and Rep 192: estates of Dommes, Berg, Müldner von Mülnheim). See also the files in the Plettenberg family archive

Chapter 10: Inside the Resistance Network

For the resistance of the military-conservative camp to Hitler:

Becker, Manuel, Löttel, Holger and Studt, Christoph (eds), *Der militärische Widerstand gegen Hitler im Lichte neuer Kontroversen: XXI. Königswinter Tagung vom 22.-24. Februar 2008* (Berlin, 2010).

Enzensberger, Hans Magnus, *Kurt von Hammerstein oder Der Eigensinn. Eine deutsche Geschichte* (Frankfurt/M., 2008).

Hassell, Ulrich von, *Die Hassell-Tagebücher 1938-1944. Aufzeichnungen vom Andern Deutschland* (Berlin 1989) (for Plettenberg pp. 269f, 358, 374, 407, 409; for Prince Louis Ferdinand pp. 272ff).

Messerschmidt, Manfred, 'Motivationen der nationalkonservativen Opposition und des militärischen Widerstands seit dem Frankreich-Feldzug', in Müller, Klaus Jürgen (ed.), *Der deutsche Widerstand 1933-1945* (Paderborn, 1986).

Müller, Klaus Jürgen, 'Der nationalkonservative Widerstand 1933-1940', in ibid. (ed.), *Der deutsche Widerstand 1933-1945* (Paderborn, 1986), pp. 40–59.

_____, *Generaloberst Ludwig Beck. Eine Biographie* (Paderborn, 2008), pp. 334–55.

Reich, Ines, *Carl Friedrich Goerdeler, Ein Bürgermeister gegen den NS-Staat* (Cologne, 1997).

Ritter, Gerhard, *Carl Goerdeler und die Deutsche Widerstandsbewegung* (Stuttgart, 1956)

Schmädeke, Jürgen, and Steinbach, Peter (eds), *Der Widerstand gegen den Nationalsozialismus* (Munich and Zurich, 1985), pp. 977–1003.

Schröder, Stephen, and Studt, Christoph (eds), *Der 20. Juli 1944 – Profile, Motive, Desiderate, XX. Königswinter Tagung vom 23.-25. Februar 2007* (Berlin, 2008).

Steinbach, Peter, 'Zum Verhältnis der Ziele des militärischen und zivilen Widerstands' in

Ueberschaer, Gerd R., 'Das Dilemma der deutschen Militäropposition', *Beiträge zum Widerstand 1933-1945* (ed. by the German Resistance Memorial Center), Issue 32 (Berlin 1988).

_____, (ed), *NS-Verbrechen und der militärische Widerstand gegen Hitler* (Darmstadt, 2000).

For the attempted overthrown of 20 July 1944:

1. Overviews and individual aspects

Berthold, Will, *Die 42 Attentate auf Adolf Hitler* (Wiesbaden, 2007).

Hamerow, Theodore S., *On the Road to the Wolf's Lair. German Resistance to Hitler* (Boston, 1997).

Hoffmann, Peter, *Widerstand-Staatstreich-Attentat* (Munich, 1979).

_____, *Claus Schenk Graf von Stauffenberg. Die Biographie* (Munich, 2007), p. 397.

_____, 'Oberst i.G. Henning von Tresckow und die Staatstreichpläne im Jahr 1943', *Vierteljahreshefte für Zeitgeschichte* (2007) 2, pp. 331–61.

Krockow, Christian Graf von, *Eine Frage der Ehre. Stauffenberg und das Hitler-Attentat vom 20. Juli 1944* (Berlin, 2002).

Lühe, Irmgard von der, *Lebenswege im Widerstand* (Hamburg, 1993), pp. 112ff.

Reich, Ines, *Potsdam und der 20. Juli 1944. Auf den Spuren des Widerstandes gegen den Nationalsozialismus* (Freiburg, 1994), pp. 49–52, 77.

Rothfels, Hans, *Die deutsche Opposition gegen Hitler. Eine Würdigung* (Zurich, 1994) (originally Frankfurt 1958).

Schultz, Hans Jürgen (ed), *Der Zwanzigste Juli – Alternative zu Hitler?* (Stuttgart, 1974). Steinbach, Peter, *Widerstand im Widerstreit* (Paderborn, 2001).

Vogel, Thomas (ed), *Aufstand des Gewissens. Militärischer Widerstand gegen Hitler und das NS-Regime 1933 bis 1945. Begleitband zur Wanderausstellung des Militärgeschichtlichen Forschungsamtes* (Hamburg, 2001).

Voß, Rüdiger von, *Der Staatstreich vom 20. Juli 1944. Politische Rezeption und Traditionsbildung in der Bundesrepublik Deutschland* (Berlin, 2011).

Zeller, Eberhard, *Geist der Freiheit. Der Zwanzigste Juli* (Munich, 1965), pp. 293, 332, 352.

2. Memories of Kurt von Plettenberg by conspirators and their relatives regarding 20 July 1944:

Bussche, Axel Freiherr von dem, *Zur Erinnerung an Kurt von Plettenberg*, Gedenkrede, Bückeburg 28 April 1985; (see also his statements in: 'Widerstand. Eine deutsche Szene', *FAZ*, December 1985).

_____, 'Eid und Schuld', in Medem, Gevinon von, *Axel von dem Bussche* (Mainz, 1994), pp 133–42.

'"Er wollte Hitler töten". Ein Portrait des Axel von dem Bussche', in Medem, Gevinon von, *Axel von dem Bussche* (Mainz, 1994), pp. 145–57.

Dönhoff, Marion Gräfin, *Um der Ehre willen. Erinnerungen an die Freunde vom 20. Juli* (Berlin, 1994).

_____, 'Axel von dem Bussche im Widerstand', in Medem, Gevinon von, *Axel von dem Bussche* (Mainz, 1994), pp. 31–5.

Falkenhausen, Gotthard Freiherr von, 'Erinnerungen, Herbst 1945', in Schramm, Wilhelm Ritter von, *Aufstand der Generale. Der 20. Juli in Paris* (Munich, 1964), pp. 29ff (see also unpublished manuscript, family archive Bettina von Falkenhausen, Essen).

Hammerstein, Kunrat von, *Spähtrupp* (Stuttgart, 1963), pp. 212, 214–16.

_____, *Flucht. Aufzeichnungen nach dem 20. Juli* (Freiburg, 1966), pp. 9, 29f, 47, 118.

Hardenberg, Carl-Hans Graf von, 'Das Wohl des Volkes verlangt den vollen Einsatz von uns. Erinnerungen an den 20. Juli 1944', in Hardenberg. Carl-Hans von, *Ein deutsches Schicksal im Widerstand*, ed. Günter Agde (Berlin, 1994), pp. 36–46, 49.

_____, 'Erlebnisbericht Sylvester 1945', in Hardenberg, Reinhild Gräfin von, *Auf immer neuen Wegen. Erinnerungen an Neuhardenberg und den Widerstand gegen den Nationalsozialismus* (Berlin, 2003), appendix pp. 163–92;

Mühleisen, Horst, 'Patrioten im Widerstand. Carl-Hans Graf von Hardenbergs Erlebnisbericht', *Vierteljahreshefte für Zeitgeschichte* 41/3 (1993), pp. 419–77, introduced and annotated by Reinhild Gräfin von Hardenberg, *Auf immer neuen Wegen. Erinnerungen an Neuhardenberg und den Widerstand gegen den Nationalsozialismus*, (Berlin, 2003), pp 100, 104.

_____, 'Ich war die Nummer 363.44', in Hardenberg, Carl-Hans von, '"Das Wohl des Volkes verlangt den vollen Einsatz von uns". Erinnerungen an den 20. Juli 1944', in von Hardenberg, Carl-Hans, *Ein deutsches Schicksal im Widerstand*, ed. Günter Agde (Berlin, 1994), pp. 180, 183.

Hielscher, Friedrich, *Fünfzig Jahre unter Deutschen* (Hamburg, 1954), pp. 333ff.

Kardorff, Ursula von, *Berliner Aufzeichnungen 1942-1945* (Munich, 1997), pp. 116, 123.

Louis Ferdinand, Prinz von Preußen, *Im Strom der Geschichte* (Bergisch-Gladbach, 1985).

Schlabrendorff, Fabian von, *Offiziere gegen Hitler* (Berlin, 1984), p. 150.

Stadie, Babette (ed), 'Die Macht der Wahrheit. Reinhold Schneiders "Gedenkwort zum 20. Juli"' in *Reaktionen von Hinterbliebenen des Widerstands* (Berlin, 2008), pp. 70ff, 145ff.

Willisen, Achim Freiherr von, *Erinnerungen*, unpublished manuscript, n.d., Plettenberg family archive

3. Further works on 20 July 1944:

Boeselager, Philipp Freiherr von, Fehrenbach, Florence and Tiffert, Reinhard, *Wir wollten Hitler töten. Ein letzter Zeuge des 20. Juli erinnert sich* (Munich, 2008).

Bottlenberg-Landsberg, *Maria Theodora von dem, Karl Ludwig Freiherr von und zu Guttenberg. 1902-1945. Ein Lebensbild* (Berlin, 2003).

Brakelmann, Günter, *Peter Yorck von Wartenburg. 1904-1944. Eine Biographie* (Munich, 2012), pp. 212.

Bruns, Wibke, *Meines Vaters Land. Geschichte einer deutschen Familie* (Munich, 2004).

Guttenberg, Karl-Ludwig Freiherr von und zu, *Tagebuchaufzeichnungen bis 1945* (family archive Theodora Freifrau von dem Bottlenberg-Landsberg)

Harpprecht, Klaus, *Die Gräfin. Marion Dönhoff. Eine Biographie* (Reinbek, 2008), pp. 103ff, 292, 323ff.

Ringshausen, Gerhard, *Hans-Alexander von Voß. Generalstabsoffizier im Widerstand. 1907-1944* (Berlin, 2008).

Schulthess, Konstanze von, *Nina Schenk Gräfin von Stauffenberg: Ein Porträt* (Munich, 2008).

Schwerin, Christoph Graf von, *Als sei nichts gewesen* (Berlin, 1997).

Vollmer, Antje, *Doppelleben: Heinrich und Gottliebe von Lehndorff im Widerstand gegen Hitler und Ribbentrop* (Frankfurt/ M, 2010).

Voß, Rüdiger von, *Hans-Alexander von Voß 1907-1944. Im Schatten der Väter* (Göttingen, 2013).

Chapter 11: After the Failure of Operation *Valkyrie*

For the wave of arrests after 20 July 1944 and for the trials before the People's Court:

Bussche, Axel Freiherr von dem, *Zur Erinnerung an Kurt von Plettenberg, Gedenkrede* (Bückeburg, 28 April 1985), pp. 10ff.

Gutermuth, Frank, and Netzbandt, Arno (eds), *Die Gestapo* (Berlin, 2006).

Hardenberg, Renate von, '"… ging ich meine schweren Gänge". Brief an Wilfried von Hardenberg, Sommer 1946', in Hardenberg, Carl-

Hans von, *Ein deutsches Schicksal im Widerstand*, ed. Günter Agde (Berlin, 1994), pp. 80–3, 94, 113.

Hett, Ulrike, and Tuchel, Johannes, 'Die Reaktionen des NS-Staates auf den Umsturzversuch vom 20. Juli 1944', in Steinbach, Peter, and Tuchel, Johannes (eds), *Widerstand gegen den nationalsozialistische Diktatur 1933-1945* (Bonn, 2004), pp. 522–34.

Hoffmann, Peter, *Widerstand-Staatstreich-Attentat* (Munich, 1979).

Stiftung Topographie des Terrors, *Das 'Hauptgefängnis' der Gestapo-Zentrale in Berlin. Terror und Widerstand 1933-1945* (Berlin, 2006).

Mühlen, Bengt von zur (ed), *Die Angeklagten des 20. Juli vor dem Volksgerichtshof* (Berlin, 2001).

Winnig, August, *Aus zwanzig Jahren. 1925 bis 1945* (Hamburg, 1951), pp. 177, 211ff.

Zeller, Eberhard, *Geist der Freiheit. Der Zwanzigste Juli* (Munich, 1965).

For the rescue of the Prussian royal crown and Frederick the Great's snuffboxes:

Files dated 12th August 1943 and 8th February 1945 in the Plettenberg family archive.

Lohmann, Dieter, 'Ein Jahr Asyl für die Krone des Hauses Preußen', in *Unsere Kirche. Evangelisches Sonntagsblatt für Westfalen und Lippe* No. 11 (10 March 1985).

'Unter der Kellertreppe', *Der Spiegel* 38 (1948).

Viktoria Luise, Herzogin von Braunschweig-Lüneburg, *Im Glanz der Krone* (Göttingen, 1967), pp. 15–17.

For the quote by René Quinton:

Quinton, René, *Die Stimme des Krieges* (Berlin-Zurich, 1936), p. 78.

Chapter 12: Denunciation

For plans after 20 July to overthrow Hitler and for the role of Ruprecht Gehring and Bernhard Horstmann:

Horstmann, Bernhard, *Prinz-Albrecht-Straße 8. Der authentische Bericht des letzten Überlebenden von 1945* (Munich 1997) (with annotations by Klaus Mayer). Manuscript dated 1947 in the Plettenberg family archive.

Kolbe, Fritz, 'Verrat als Waffe', *Spiegel Online* (30 January 2011).

Mayer, Klaus, *Zwischenbericht zur Forschungsaarbeit über Oberleutnant Ruprecht Gehring (1920–1945) et al* (unpublished manuscript, Berlin, 2005).

Nippert, Erwin, *Prinz-Albrecht-Straße 8* (Berlin, 1990), pp. 186ff.

Schulenburg, Tisa Gräfin von der, *Ich hab's gewagt – Bildhauerin und*

Ordensfrau – ein unkonventionelles Leben (Freiburg i.Br., 1981).

Speer, Albert, *Inside the Third Reich* (New York, 1997), pp. 436ff.

Stehle, Hans Jakob, 'Der Mann, der den Krieg verkürzen wollte' (on Fritz Kolbe), in *DIE ZEIT* no. 9 (2 May 1986), p. 35.

For Bernhard Horstmann:

The response by the Federal Archive Berlin (dated 2 March 2011) to the author's query regarding Bernhard Horstmann's membership in Nazi organisations yielded information on his Hitler Youth and NSDAP membership (membership no. 5504246 dated 1st September 1937). Furthermore it is written: 'The arrest due to his resistance activities by the Gestapo could not be verified through research in various individual-related archives or in the stock R58 of the Reich Security Main Office.'

The Wehrmacht Inquiries Office in Berlin provided details of his military career from 1 September 1939 in a letter dated 11 March 2011 (troop units, war captivity and ranks).

For Hitler's relationship with the Hohenzollerns:

Domarus, Max, *Hitler, Reden und Proklamationen* (Wiesbaden, 1973), Vol. II, 1, pp. 1476ff, 1888, 2035, 2127.

Friedrich Wilhelm Prinz von Preußen, *Die Hohenzollern und der Nationalsozialismus*, PhD Thesis at the Ludwig-Maximilian-University (Munich, 1983), pp. 394–455.

Fröhlich, Elke (ed), *Die Tagebücher von Joseph Goebbels* (Munich 1997–2005), Tagebuch II, pp. 170, 241, 621.

Hassell, Ulrich von, *Die Hassell-Tagebücher 1938-1944. Aufzeichnungen vom Anderen Deutschland* (Berlin, 1989), pp. 272ff, 490 (fn. 104).

Jonas, Klaus W., *Der Kronprinz Wilhelm* (Frankfurt/ M., 1962).

Louis Ferdinand Prinz von Preußen, *Die Geschichte meines Lebens* (Göttingen, 1969), pp. 122ff, 187ff, 256ff, 288–302 (for Plettenberg: p. 314).

_____, *Im Strom der Geschichte* (Munich–Vienna, 1983).

Picker, Henry, *Hitlers Tischgespräche* (Stuttgart, 1976), p. 418.

Ritter, Gerhard, *Carl Goerdeler und die deutsche Widerstandsbewegung* (Stuttgart, 1964), p. 550.

Schroeder, Christa, *He Was My Chief: The Memoirs of Adolf Hitler's Secretary* (Barnsley, 2009).

Viktoria Luise, Herzogin von Braunschweig-Lüneburg, *Im Strom der Zeit* (Göttingen, 1974), p. 292.

Zoller, Albert, *Hitler privat. Erlebnisbericht seiner Geheimsekretärin*

(Düsseldorf, 1949), p. 186 (the book is based on a manuscript by Christa Schroeder and on interviews with her).

Chapter 13: Prinz-Albrecht-Straße 8

For the Gestapo prison at Prinz-Albrecht-Straße 8:

Rürup, Reinhard, *Topographie des Terrors* (Berlin, 1991).

Topography of Terror Foundation, *Das 'Hausgefängnis' der Gestapo-Zentrale in Berlin. Terror und Widerstand 1933-1945* (Berlin, 2006).

Tuchel, Johannes, and Schattenfroh, Reinhold, *Zentrale des Terrors. Prinz-Albrecht-Straße 8* (Berlin, 1987) (for Plettenberg p. 289).

Zipfel, Friedrich, 'Gestapo and SD in Berlin', in Berger, Wilhelm, and Carl Hinrichs (eds), *Jahrbuch für die Geschichte Mittel- und Ostdeutschlands* Vol. IX/X (Tübingen, 1961), pp. 263–92.

The memoirs of the Reich Minister of Finance Lutz Count Schwerin von Krosigk:

Schwerin von Krosigk, Lutz Graf, *Staatsbankrott* (Göttingen, 1974), pp. 343ff.

On Plettenberg's last journey to Mittelberg-Baad:

Jonas, Klaus W., *Der Kronprinz Wilhelm* (Frankfurt/M., 1962), p. 282.

Louis Ferdinand, Prinz von Preußen, *Die Geschichte meines Lebens* (Göttingen, 1968), p. 314.

Letters by Privy Councillor Arthur Berg to the Crown Prince dated 15 March and 26 March 1945:

Berg estate in the Secret Prussian State Archive in Berlin-Dahlem

The quote from the book *Gedanken sind Kräfte*:

March, Werner, *Gedanken sind Kräfte* (Berlin, 1942).

Epilogue: 'Greater love hath no man than this, that a man lay down his life for his friends'

For the Bornstedt cemetery:

Kunzendorf, Gottfried, and Richter, Manfred (eds), *Bornstedt Friedhof Kirche* (Berlin, 2001).

Plümecke, Klaus Ingo, *Potsdam 400 Jahre Bornstedter Friedhof. Licht und Schatten hinter Sanssouci* (Cologne, 1998).

Reich, Ines, *Potsdam und der 20. Juli 1944* (Freiburg, 1994).

For the commemoration of Kurt von Plettenberg:

Bussche, Axel Freiherr von dem, *Zur Erinnerung an Kurt von Plettenberg*, memorial address,

Bückeburg, 28 April 1985, p. 2.

Hardenberg, Carl-Hans von, *Ein deutsches Schicksal im Widerstand*, ed. Günter Agde, (Berlin, 1994), p. 50.

Museumseisenbahn, Die. *Zeitschrift für Freunde der Dampf-Eisenbahn* 3/1991, Bruchhausen-Vilsen (report on the speech by Prince Louis Ferdinand regarding the naming of 'Plettenberg').

Index